D1551994

# the greek cook

**simple seasonal food**

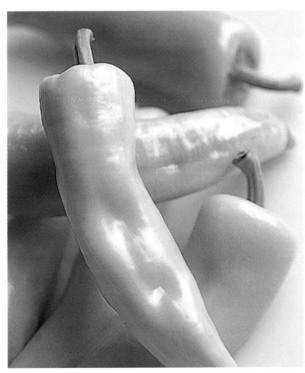

# rena salaman
# the greek cook
## simple seasonal food

aquamarine

photographs by martin brigdale

for Alexandra and Sophie

# contents

# introduction

the essence of Greek cuisine is its
simplicity – the dishes may sometimes be frugal,
but they are always wonderfully flavoured

**Left**
Greeks love all kinds of seafood, from shellfish such as mussels to fish such as red gurnard. The best quality fish is simply grilled, while shellfish and the popular squid and cuttlefish are made into delicious pilaffs and substantial, warming casseroles.

**When I was growing up** in Athens in the 1950s, the most eagerly awaited arrival every morning was the horse-drawn cart of the vegetable seller, who advertised his wares in a loud, hoarse voice that drew all the women in the vicinity like bees. Nowadays, when I go to Athens to visit my sister in Glyfada, one of my main pleasures (after looking at the wonderful shoe shops there) is going twice a week to the two street markets near her home. Vegetables, glowing with freshness, are brought to market by the growers and arranged in colourful piles along the street, as in a neat parade.

On the islands that are often too barren to support much agriculture, the arrival of fresh supplies of fruit and vegetables is even more eagerly anticipated. On my summer visits to Alonnisos, I am as eager as anyone for the twice-weekly visit of the *Evangelistria*, the large, wide-bodied caique, painted in the colours of the Greek flag – cobalt blue on the hull, with a broad white stripe above – which carries provisions to the island from the picturesque mainland port of Volos. Although the provisions may include building materials, furniture, manure, plants, even keys that have been copied as extras (Panagiotis, the handsome

captain of the *Evangelistria* being a very reliable man who willingly accepts commissions of this nature), it is the cargo of fresh vegetables and fruit that generates the most excitement.

Islanders rejoice at the prospect of all those shining courgettes (zucchini) and regal purple aubergines (eggplant), the green beans of all kinds, the okra, the fat, sweet tomatoes and the light-green long peppers that are indispensable for that Pelion speciality, spetzofai.

Depending on the season, Panagiotis may also bring perfumed white peaches from Katerini, huge purple cherries from Edessa in the north, juicy nectarines, melons from Crete, and many more delights, all eagerly anticipated by the watchers on the shore.

If this seems a little exaggerated, it is not. Greek cuisine is centred around vegetables and other simple, fresh ingredients – and quality produce is at its heart.

**Right**
A brightly painted wooden fishing boat is anchored alongside the local café on the quay in the tiny port of one of the many Aegean islands.

## Ancient connections

A preoccupation with good produce does not simply apply to the modern Greek diet. The Greek culinary tradition has its origins in antiquity, and classical authors describe a number of vegetable-based dishes that are still popular today. Skorthalia (a rich garlic sauce made with olive oil and bread), fava (a thick and tasty purée of yellow split peas) and dolmathes (fresh vine leaves stuffed with rice and herbs), for instance, have changed little since they were the favoured foods of the ancient Greeks.

Aristophanes, the Athenian playwright who lived from 448 to 388 BC, makes satirical comments in his plays about the popularity of pulses. Broad beans, lentils, chickpeas and split peas were as popular then as they are now. The ancient dish *etnos*, which he describes as being sold in huge cauldrons in the streets of Athens, sounds similar to modern fava. Homer describes in the Odyssey the feasts that Odysseus and his men enjoyed: barbecuing meat sprinkled with herbs – undoubtedly rigani (oregano) and thymari (thyme) – from the hillsides on Circe's island. These feasts of Odysseus were, however, special celebratory events. The ancient Greeks only ate meat when they offered sacrifices to the gods, so meat-eating was closely linked to religious observance, just as it is in modern Greece. The calendar of the Greek Orthodox Church is liberally sprinkled with long fasting periods, each of which culminates in a huge feast that invariably involves meat – preferably lamb, spit-roasted and sprinkled with wild herbs – exactly as in the Odyssey.

## Sea harvest

Of course, those who have access to the sea also have access to wonderful fish and shellfish, another favourite subject of the ancient Greek writers. Both Athenaeus in his *Deipnosophistae* (Banquet of the Learned) and the poet Archestratus in *Hedypatheia* (The Life of Luxury) wrote at some length about seafood, and included hints about where to find the best quality fish and how to cook it. Archestratus adopted a light approach. His favourite methods were boiling, roasting or grilling fish with seasoning and olive oil. In their 1994 translation of Archestratus' famous work, which they describe as "Europe's Oldest Cookery Book", John Wilkins and Shaun Hill write that "sauces of cheese or herb pickles are added to inferior fish, the preference being for additions of oil and light herbs to the fish juices". Not so very different from the olive oil, lemon and oregano sauce that accompanies most fish dishes in Greece today.

Apart from top quality fish, which is mostly grilled or made into fish soups, Greeks make good use of all kinds of fish and shellfish.

**Below**
This vegetable vendor from Astypalea transports his produce from village to village on the backs of two mules. In his hand is his portable weighing machine.

Squid and small cuttlefish are often fried until crisp and offered as mezethes. They are also made into substantial casseroles, like squid with spinach or cuttlefish with potatoes.

## A simple diet

Greece is a small country bordering the eastern end of the Mediterranean sea. Mainland Greece occupies the southern part of the Balkan peninsula, and there are numerous islands in the Ionian and Aegean seas. The frugal diet, based on simply cooked fresh ingredients, can be explained by various factors, but is largely determined by the hilly terrain and the arid climate. Greece's history has not helped either, as it has been rather turbulent, culminating in the 20th century with the German Occupation in 1941 and the subsequent Civil War.

The disruption of trade through conflict, coupled with the limited resources of the land, meant that Greeks have had to use their imagination to transform what little they had into interesting and varied dishes. Just how well they succeed is illustrated by the recipes in this collection. Frugal the diet may be, but it is by no means boring. Colourful stuffed vegetables

**Above**
Although the islands are often too barren to support much agriculture, fresh sheep's cheeses and the much-loved large green olives are still produced.

**Right**
A favourite meze: tentacles and rings of squid, fried until crisp.

and vine leaves, delicious stews, grilled fish and meat kebabs and crisp filo pies are just a few of the wonderful dishes to be enjoyed.

## The Greek table

Meals in Greece are often loosely arranged affairs, not set for prescribed times or regulated by any particular number of courses. Greeks are not keen on breakfast, apart from a small Greek coffee or tea with lemon. Mid-morning snacks could be either a sesame-studded koulouri or a hot cheese pie, tyropitta, from the corner street seller. Lunch in typical Mediterranean fashion is served late and the main meal of the day will be dinner, which is also served late.

When Greeks go out to eat, which they do a lot, they seldom arrive at the restaurant before 10 p.m. Pre-dinner drinks such as ouzo can be accompanied by very simple mezethes, such as shiny olives and feta cheese, or something more esoteric like the preserved caper leaves that they serve on the island of Santorini. Dinner can be made up altogether by mezethes, which everyone around the table shares, then if there is something really tantalizing, and there is still a little space left for it, you may like to order one or two main dishes to be shared by all again. This is the most wonderful way of eating and it's

what we always do at my favourite restaurant in Athens, Vlassis, where the stuffed cabbage leaves and fava are unsurpassed.

Although Greeks are not heavy drinkers, wine is always drunk with meals. Nowadays, the traditional wine, retsina, is being replaced by non-resinated varieties and there are excellent new wines on the market; a few of them shyly making an appearance abroad. Look out for those from the vineyards of Skouras, Strofylia and Hadzimichalis.

### The golden liquid

There is one ingredient without which Greek and indeed all Mediterranean cooking would be very impoverished. This is olive oil, the glorious golden liquid that gives Greek cooking its distinct richness of flavour. There is scarcely a dish that is not ennobled by it, from dips to desserts. It breathes life into vegetables and pulses, makes salads superb and is an essential ingredient in most meat and fish dishes. Olive oil is part of Greek social history, politics and folklore, and life is unimaginable without it.

Greek olive oil is mostly dark green in colour and has a very fruity flavour. It is usually smooth with sweet undertones, but occasionally it is

**Above**
In Greece, wine is always drunk with meals and occasionally used in cooking.

**Right**
Golden-coloured Greek olive oil has a wonderfully fruity flavour.

grassy, like the olive oils of Tuscany. It is one of the best in the Mediterrranean yet paradoxically one of the cheapest. There are excellent examples worth seeking out and trying, such as Iliada and the wonderful Mani (particularly the organic version) or Kolymbari from Crete.

Apart from its taste, there is also the question of the role of olive oil in nutrition and good health. When I was growing up, research into olive oil was in its infancy. So while it was common knowledge that olive oil was good for our skin, our teeth, our bones and our eyes – as my grandmother told us every day – we did not know then what we know now. We did not know that olive oil is low in saturated fatty acids, which raise cholesterol levels in the blood. Nor were we aware of its high content of polyunsaturated and mono-unsaturated fatty acids, which lower levels of harmful cholesterol.

However, I could not end this introduction to Greek cooking on such a sensible and serious note. This would be far from the playful character of Greek cuisine, which is epitomized by long, happy lunches under the olive trees and consumed in the unique conviviality that is, in itself, the best witness to the spirit of Greek food.

*Rena Salaman*

# spring

new leaves, fresh vegetables and glorious fish and shellfish

**You can tell** that spring is in the air, not only by the riot of roses on every fence and the enchanting scent of the blossom on the orange and lemon trees, but also by what is going on in the kitchen. Spring spells the end of the slow-simmered casseroles, the dried beans, chickpeas and hearty meat stews. The kitchen literally acquires a lighter character as the sun gets warmer and the days get longer. By the end of February there is hope in the air. There is a Greek proverb which goes: *O Flevaris kian Flevisi kalokeri tha myrisi* (No matter how bad February can become, it will always bring the scent of summer).

The first trees to flower are the almonds, around the end of February or the beginning of March, and by then spring is well on the way. At the local street markets and greengrocers, accurate barometers of the seasons, the first globe artichokes begin to appear, either spilled in unruly heaps on rugs or beautifully arranged. Shiny spring onions (scallions) will be set like suitors beside them, and there will also be bunches of feathery dill, all indispensable for spring dishes such as artichokes with potatoes. As the season proceeds, the first tender broad beans appear, to be followed in late April by tender, sweet peas. These are cooked with artichokes in countless combinations in the weeks that follow, and are so much a part of Greek tradition that I can smell spring whenever I cook artichokes, even in the middle of winter.

Spring is the season that includes the longest fasting period in the Christian Church – particularly the Greek Orthodox Church. This is Lent, when worshippers abstain from eating meat and dairy products, and salt cod enters the spring menu. Traditionally, this dried fish is always eaten on 25 March, the day of the Annunciation of the Virgin Mary. It is soaked, then dipped in batter and fried before being served with skorthalia, the fiery garlic sauce that can revive the most faded palate. Salt cod is also baked with potatoes and garlic, and it is often served this way on Fridays during Lent.

Salt cod is not the only Lenten ingredient. Fish of all kinds is served in place of meat, and seafood such as squid, cuttlefish and octopus are combined with rice, pasta, potatoes, spinach or wild greens and made into substantial family dishes. On Palm Sunday, fish is eaten in every Greek household, either baked, grilled or as fish soup.

**Left**
Globe artichokes are one of the most popular vegetables in Greece. When very young, the hearts are thinly sliced raw into salads, while older specimens are slow-cooked in casseroles.

**Above**
The fragrant flavour of early garlic is used to perfection in Greek cooking: tiny slivers are pressed into spring lamb before roasting or whole and unpeeled cloves are baked with chicken.

The wild greens that are used in fish and shellfish dishes have other uses, too. In the countryside, this is the season for spring pies. Although pies can be made with spinach or leeks and cheese in the winter, it is in the spring that some of the most delicious pies are made. They are flavoured with wild greens and herbs from the hillsides, such as tender poppy leaves, picked before the plants have begun to flower.

The most glorious event in spring – and the highlight of the Greek Orthodox calendar – is Easter. Holy Week is a period of strict fasting. No meat, fish or dairy products may be eaten, and the evenings are given over to churchgoing. The long, but melodious liturgy on Saturday evening culminates at midnight with the singing of the Byzantine hymn, Christ has Risen, by priests resplendent in golden robes. Their jewel-studded crowns sparkle in the light of the candles held by the congregation. Everyone brings a scarlet hard-boiled egg, and it is the cracking of these against the eggs of relatives and friends that signifies that the fast is broken.

The climax comes with Easter lunch, a celebration with its roots in pagan ritual. In gardens, baby lambs and goats are slowly

spit-roasted. At this time of year, their meat is quite delectable. Delicacies include kokoretsi, sausage-like preparations made from the lamb intestines, liver, lights, heart and spleen.

In the days following Easter, dishes such as lamb and cos lettuce fricassée make their appearance. Flavoured with dill and bound with an egg and lemon sauce, this is absolutely delicious, as is lamb with artichokes or peas. Small legs of lamb are roasted with potatoes and garlic. After all the fasting, lamb is eaten at every opportunity.

May brings the first tender vine leaves, and it is then that one of the best dishes in Greek cuisine is made – dolmathes. As this is also the season of herbs, such as the feathery wild fennel that appears by the roadsides, it is no surprise that the very best version of these tasty stuffed vine leaves is a vegetarian one, with masses of onions, spring onions and herbs. On the island of Alonnisos they also use young sorrel leaves in the stuffing – and Alonnisian dolmathes are the best that I have ever tried.

As the days get warmer, the first beans and aubergines appear, and you know that the most glorious season of all – summer – is just around the corner.

**Many of the ingredients** that are essential in Greek cookery are available all year, but some are distinctly seasonal. Their arrival is eagerly anticipated, not merely because they mark the passage of time, but also because they play such a vital role in dishes that have for centuries been made to mark specific occasions. Spring ingredients are perhaps the most precious of all, since their appearance in markets and gardens indicates the beginning of another cycle in the culinary calendar.

### Peas and fresh broad beans

Young peas play an important role in spring dishes in Greece. They are made into substantial casseroles, often combined with globe artichokes and fresh, feathery dill, or with lamb and baby courgettes. It is not unusual to see whole families shelling peas, or splitting fleshy broad bean pods to release the beans inside. Some recipes call for the tender inner broad beans, that are a beautiful, bright green, and taste delicious.

### Garlic

This aromatic bulb is indispensable to Greek food and, along with oregano, thyme and dill, is one of the primary ingredients. It is added generously to dishes that are to be cooked, but it is also used raw in sauces such as skorthalia or eaten raw with robust winter soups.

### Vine leaves

Many Greek houses have their own grape vines, and cooks make good use of the leaves. The first, tender leaves are picked in May, which is when they also appear in the markets. Leaves that are to be used immediately must be rinsed, then blanched in boiling water for a few minutes. If the leaves are to be stored for any length of time, they can be packed raw in small bundles in a container and frozen. When needed, the frozen leaves are plunged into boiling water for 1–2 minutes, then drained.

The primary purpose for which vine leaves are used in Greece is in the making of dolmathes. The leaves are rolled around rice-based

**Left**
Entire Greek families can often be seen sitting in the spring sunshine shelling freshly picked broad beans.

**Above**
Essential Greek ingredients: vine leaves are stuffed to make dolmathes, while garlic is often used as a flavouring.

**Opposite**
Spring ingredients, clockwise from top left: dandelion leaves, globe artichokes, spring onions, cos lettuce and fresh oregano.

vegetarian or meat fillings, then layered in a pan and cooked with olive oil and lemon juice. It is important to use large quantities of finely chopped onions and plenty of aromatic fresh herbs with the rice, and generous amounts of extra virgin olive oil.

Vine leaves are also used to wrap fish for baking or grilling. They impart a lovely, lemony aroma and flavour to the fish. If you haven't a supply of fresh vine leaves, then preserved vine leaves in brine, which are sold in vacuum packs can be used. However, they tend to be salty, so rinse them carefully before use.

### Globe artichokes

The artichoke is a cultivated variety of the cardoon and the thistle, that was developed in 15th-century Italy. It soon spread to other Mediterranean countries and is very popular in Greece. Its arrival in local markets signals the start of spring.

Young artichokes can be eaten raw. The hearts are thinly sliced into salads, and the vegetable is also cooked in casseroles with other spring vegetables or spring lamb.

### Preparing artichokes

• Cut artichokes discolour readily, so you need to begin by preparing a bowl of acidulated water. Fill a bowl with cold water and add the juice of half a lemon.

• Remove and discard the outer leaves of the artichoke until you reach the tender ones. Cut off the head of the artichoke, halfway down, leaving the heart with a short collar of tender leaves.
• Slice the artichoke in half lengthways, using a sharp knife, so that you can see the hairy choke in the middle of the heart, surrounded by small, hard purple leaves. Scoop this out with a stainless steel teaspoon and throw it away.
• Cut off the stalk, leaving about 4cm/1½in attached to the artichoke. Peel away the woody green outer surface from the attached piece of stalk and base and pull away any small base leaves. Drop the artichoke into the bowl of acidulated water until you are ready to cook it.

**Left**
In Greek markets, the presence of young globe artichokes, which are often cooked in casseroles with other vegetables like peas, signals the arrival of spring.

## Dill

Greek cooks love fresh dill and they will often use whole bunches of it to flavour a single casserole. The feathery herb is native to the Mediterranean area and grows wild on the hillsides in Greece. Since ancient times, it has been used extensively in Greek cooking, and the unmistakable aroma adds character to all the spring dishes, especially dolmathes (stuffed vine leaves). A member of the parsley family, dill is a very similar herb to fennel, but is much smaller. It has a refreshing, light anise taste, resembling that of caraway, but is not as strong.

## Salt cod

The elegant, opaque sides of salt cod are always associated with the end of Carnival and the beginning of Lent, usually around the end of February. In the 40 days that follow, salt cod is served, particularly on Fridays, in all sorts of delicious dishes. It is baked with potatoes and dill; made into croquettes; or fried and served with skorthalia, the delicious Greek garlic sauce. Salt cod must be soaked in cold water for at least 24 hours before being cooked. It is important to change the water frequently, to extract as much salt as possible.

**Left**
Greek yogurt is thick and creamy and the best has a slightly sharp flavour, neither insipid nor immensely sour.

**Below**
Salt cod, a favourite of the Greeks during Lent, is good cooked with potatoes, tomatoes, herbs and olives.

## Greek yogurt

Proper Greek yogurt is deliciously thick and creamy and has a lacy crust on top. This is the yogurt that I remember from my childhood, when a wandering seller would come to our door every evening. A thick slice of creamy white yogurt would be cut from the contents of his flat terracotta container and weighed.

Yogurt like this can still be found, produced by traditionally run firms, particularily in towns such as Volos, Larissa, Kalamata or cosmopolitan Thessalonica. The best yogurt of this kind I have ever tasted was on Crete, and it is well worth seeking out if you visit the island. Greeks love to eat yogurt with thyme-scented honey spooned on top as a mid-morning or late-night snack. It is one of the simplest pleasures in the world.

500g/1¼lb courgettes (zucchini)
120ml/4fl oz/½ cup extra virgin olive oil
1 large onion, finely chopped
2 spring onions (scallions), green and
    white parts finely chopped
1 garlic clove, crushed
3 medium slices of proper bread
    (not from a pre-sliced loaf)
2 eggs, lightly beaten
200g/7oz feta cheese, crumbled
50g/2oz/½ cup freshly grated Greek
    Graviera or Italian Parmesan cheese
45–60ml/3–4 tbsp finely chopped fresh
    dill or 5ml/1 tsp dried oregano
50g/2oz/½ cup plain (all-purpose) flour
salt and ground black pepper
6 lemon wedges, to serve

**Serves 6 as a snack**

# courgette rissoles from alonnisos
## kolokythokeftethes alonnisou

I had never eaten kolokythokeftethes before going to the island of Alonnisos. They are an ingenious way of transforming bland-tasting courgettes into a sharply appetizing dish that captivates everyone who tries it. These can be served as part of the meze or as a light meal, with salad.

**1** Bring a pan of lightly salted water to the boil. Slice the courgettes into 4cm/1½in lengths and drop them into the boiling water. Cover and cook for about 10 minutes, or until very soft. Drain in a colander and let them cool completely.

**2** Heat 45ml/3 tbsp of the olive oil in a frying pan, add the onion and spring onions and sauté until translucent. Add the garlic, then, as soon as it becomes aromatic, take the pan off the heat.

**3** Squeeze the courgettes with your hands, to extract as much water as possible, then place them in a large bowl. Add the fried onion and garlic mixture and mix well.

**4** Toast the bread, cut off and discard the crusts, then break up the toast and crumb it in a food processor. Add the crumbs to the courgette mixture, with the eggs, feta, grated Graviera or Parmesan.

**5** Stir in the dill or oregano and add salt and pepper to taste. Mix well, using your hands to squeeze the mixture and make sure that all the ingredients are combined evenly. If the courgette mixture seems too wet, add a little flour.

**6** Take about a heaped tablespoon of the courgette mixture, roll it into a round ball and press it lightly to make the typical rissole shape. Make more rissoles in the same way.

**7** Coat the rissoles lightly in the flour and dust off any excess. Heat the remaining olive oil in a large non-stick frying pan and fry the rissoles, in batches if necessary, until they are crisp and brown, turning them over once or twice during cooking. Drain the rissoles on a double layer of kitchen paper and serve on a warmed platter, with the lemon wedges.

900g/2lb medium squid
50g/2oz/½ cup plain (all-purpose) flour
75ml/5 tbsp olive oil or sunflower oil,
   for frying
large pinch of dried oregano
salt and ground black pepper
1 lemon, quartered, to serve

**Serves 4**

# fried squid
## kalamarakia tiganita

There are few foods more appetizing than fried squid, especially when it is enjoyed under an olive tree on the edge of a dazzling beach. And if the squid has been caught the night before, close to the coast, as it has on Alonnisos in the summer, it is a gastronomic treat. When we visit the island, plate after plate arrives on our restaurant table. The squid comes straight from the frying pan, with its tentacles crisp and scorched.

In Greece, squid is generally rolled in flour and shallow-fried. There's an art to this, as the olive oil has to be at precisely the right temperature to keep the squid tender and moist.

Fried squid can be served as a meze with salad or can accompany a soup or vegetable casserole.

1 Prepare the squid, following the instructions in the introduction to the winter chapter, but do not slit the bodies open. Having emptied the squid of all their innards, rinse the bodies thoroughly, inside and out, then drain well. Slice the bodies into 3–4cm/1¼–1½in wide rings.

2 Season the flour with salt and pepper and put it in a large plastic bag. Add the squid, keeping the rings and tentacles separate, and toss until evenly coated. Shake off any excess flour.

3 Heat the oil in a large heavy or non-stick frying pan over a medium heat. When it is hot enough to sizzle, but is not smoking, add a batch of squid rings. They should fill the pan but not touch each other.

4 Let the squid rings cook for 2–3 minutes or until pale golden, then use a fork to turn each piece over. This is a laborious process but worthwhile. Let each ring cook for 1–2 minutes more, until pale golden, then lift out with a slotted spoon and drain on a platter lined with kitchen paper.

5 Continue to cook the squid, but leave the floured tentacles to last, and take care, as they spit spitefully. The tentacles will need very little cooking as the oil will have become quite hot and they will become crisp almost immediately. Turn them over after 1 minute and take them out as soon as they are crisp and golden all over.

6 Serve the fried squid on a large warmed platter and sprinkle some dried oregano on top. Surround the pieces with the lemon wedges and invite guests to squeeze a little lemon juice over each portion.

**Ask your fishmonger**
A good fishmonger will prepare the squid for you, especially if you give him or her a little notice.

1.5 litres/2½ pints/6¼ cups water
    or fish stock
75–90ml/5–6 tbsp extra virgin olive oil
2kg/4½lb whole fish (see tip below),
    cleaned and scaled
8 small potatoes, peeled and left whole
8 small onions, peeled and left whole
2 carrots, peeled and cut into
    5cm/2in lengths
1–2 celery sticks, including some leaves
2 courgettes (zucchini), quartered
    lengthways
juice of 1 lemon
salt and ground black pepper
extra virgin olive oil, juice of 1 lemon and a
    pinch of dried oregano, to serve

**Serves 4**

# fish soup
psarosoupa

Fish in Greece is glorious. If you are standing on the quayside when a fishing boat returns to an island harbour in the morning, you may be astounded at the number and variety of fish caught, and marvel at their glistening colours and shapes.

Fish soup in Greece makes a complete meal. The liquid soup is served first, followed by a platter of the fish and vegetables from the pot. In Greece, the favoured fish would be the bright orange Mediterranean scorpionfish – the French rascasse rouge – which is also the main ingredient for the Provençal bouillabaisse. Its huge, rather ugly head adds a lot of flavour to the broth, and its bones have a glutinous quality, which is indispensable to a good fish soup. Red gurnard is a good alternative. It has a fine, sweet taste.

**1** Mix the water or stock and olive oil in a large pan. Bring to the boil, and boil rapidly for about 4 minutes in order to emulsify the liquid. Add the fish to the pan, with salt and pepper. Slowly let the liquid return to the boil and, using a slotted spoon, carefully skim the surface until it is clear.

**2** Add the potatoes, onions, carrots, celery sticks and leaves and courgettes to the pan with a little more hot water, if needed, to cover.

**3** Put a lid on the pan and cook over a medium heat until the fish is cooked and the flesh flakes when tested with the tip of a sharp knife. Large fish will take up to 35 minutes; smaller ones a little less. Make sure that the fish does not disintegrate.

**4** Carefully lift the fish out of the pan and place it on a warm platter. Scoop out the hot vegetables with a draining spoon and arrange them around the fish. Cover and keep hot.

**5** Stir the lemon juice into the soup. Serve it first, then bring out the platter of fish and vegetables. Invite guests to help themselves to a piece of fish and a selection of vegetables. Quickly whisk the olive oil with the lemon juice and oregano. This makes an excellent dressing for the fish and vegetables.

### Choose two or three fish varieties
It is possible to make this soup from just one type of fish, but you will achieve better results if you use two or three different varieties. In addition to red gurnard, try grey mullet, sea bass or snapper.

4 globe artichokes
juice of 1½ lemons
150ml/¼ pint/⅔ cup extra virgin olive oil
1 large onion, thinly sliced
3 carrots, sliced into long batons
300ml/½ pint/1¼ cups hot water
400g/14oz small new potatoes,
    scrubbed or peeled
4–5 spring onions (scallions), chopped
60–75ml/4–5 tbsp chopped fresh dill
salt and ground black pepper

**Serves 4 as a first course**

# artichokes with new potatoes
anginares a la polita

Artichokes are among the first spring
vegetables and appear in Greece in the
middle of March, together with fresh broad
beans and aromatic bunches of dill. Artichokes
are cooked in various combinations with many
spring vegetables but cooked with the new
season's potatoes they make one of the
finest vegetable dishes in the world.

**1** Prepare the artichokes, following the
instructions in the introduction to this chapter.
Drop them into a bowl of water acidulated with
about one-third of the lemon juice.

**2** Heat the olive oil in a wide, heavy pan and
sauté the onion slices gently until they become
translucent. Next add the carrots and sauté
them for 2–3 minutes. Add the remaining lemon
juice and the hot water and bring to the boil.

**3** Drain the artichokes and add them to the
pan with the potatoes, spring onions and
seasoning. The vegetables should be almost
covered with the sauce, so add a little more hot
water if needed. Cover and cook gently for
40–45 minutes. Sprinkle the dill over the top
and cook for 2–3 minutes more.

4 globe artichokes
juice of 1½ lemons
150ml/¼ pint/⅔ cup extra virgin olive oil
1 onion, thinly sliced
4–5 spring onions (scallions),
   roughly chopped
2 carrots, sliced in rounds
1.2kg/2½lb fresh peas in pods, shelled
   (this will give you about 500–675g/
   1¼–1½lb peas)
450ml/¾ pint/scant 2 cups hot water
60ml/4 tbsp finely chopped fresh dill
salt and ground black pepper

**Serves 4**

# braised artichokes with fresh peas
araka me anginares

**This artichoke dish has a unique delicacy.
Shelling fresh peas is a little time-consuming
but their matchless flavour makes the task
very worthwhile. Sit on a step outside in the
sunshine, and what at first seems a chore
will be positively sybaritic.**

**1** First, prepare the artichokes, following the
instructions in the introduction to this chapter.
Drop them into a bowl of water acidulated with
about one-third of the lemon juice.

**2** Heat the olive oil in a wide, shallow pan and add
the onion and spring onions, and then a minute
later, add the carrots. Sauté the mixture, stirring
constantly, for a few seconds, then add the peas
and stir for 1–2 minutes to coat them in the oil.

**3** Pour in the remaining lemon juice. Let it
bubble and evaporate for a few seconds, then
add the hot water and bring to the boil. Drain
the artichokes and add them to the pan, with
salt and pepper to taste. Cover and cook gently
for about 40–45 minutes, stirring occasionally.
Add the dill and cook for 5 minutes more, or
until the vegetables are beautifully tender. Serve
hot or at room temperature.

500g/1¼lb small new potatoes
5 spring onions (scallions), green and
    white parts, finely chopped
15ml/1 tbsp rinsed bottled capers
8–10 black olives
115g/4oz feta cheese, cut into small cubes
45ml/3 tbsp finely chopped fresh flat
    leaf parsley
30ml/2 tbsp finely chopped fresh mint
salt and ground black pepper

### For the vinaigrette
90–120ml/6–8 tbsp extra virgin olive oil
juice of 1 lemon, or to taste
2 salted or preserved anchovies,
    rinsed and finely chopped
45ml/3 tbsp Greek (strained plain) yogurt
45ml/3 tbsp finely chopped fresh dill
5ml/1 tsp French mustard

**Serves 4**

# potato and feta salad
patates salata me feta

A potato salad may sound mundane but this one is not, as it is redolent with the aromas of the herbs and has layer upon layer of flavours. It is an easy dish to assemble, so makes a perfect lunch or dinner for a busy day. Serve it on its own, or as a second course after one of the bean or lentil soups in this book.

Potatoes in Greece are very sweet and tasty. Look for a flavoursome salad variety like Charlotte; it will make all the difference.

**1** Bring a pan of lightly salted water to the boil and cook the potatoes in their skins for 25–30 minutes, until tender. Take care not to let them become soggy and disintegrate. Drain them thoroughly and let them cool a little.

**2** When the potatoes are cool enough to handle, peel them and place in a large bowl. If they are very small, keep them whole; otherwise cut them in large cubes. Add the spring onions, capers, olives, feta and fresh herbs and toss gently to mix.

**3** To make the vinaigrette, place the oil in a bowl with the lemon juice and anchovies.

**4** Whisk thoroughly until the dressing emulsifies and thickens. Whisk in the yogurt, dill and mustard, with salt and pepper to taste.

**5** Dress the salad while the potatoes are still warm, tossing lightly to coat everything in the delicious anchovy vinaigrette.

### Allow the flavours to develop
The salad tastes better if it has had time to sit for an hour or so at room temperature and absorb all the flavours before it is served. Any leftover salad will be delicious the next day, but take it out of the refrigerator about an hour before it is to be served or the flavours will be dulled.

50 fresh or 225g/8oz preserved vine leaves
175g/6oz/scant 1 cup long grain rice
350g/12oz onions, very finely diced
4–5 spring onions (scallions), green and
    white parts, thinly sliced
30ml/2 tbsp pine nuts, toasted
60ml/4 tbsp finely chopped fresh dill
45ml/3 tbsp finely chopped fresh mint
30ml/2 tbsp finely chopped fresh
    flat leaf parsley
150ml/¼ pint/⅔ cup extra virgin olive oil
juice of 1 lemon
450ml/¾ pint/scant 2 cups hot water
salt and ground black pepper
4–6 lemon wedges, to serve

**Serves 4 as a main course
6 as a first course**

# stuffed vine leaves with rice and spring herbs

dolmathes

These well-known and popular treats can be made with different stuffings and occasionally include meat. My favourite version is this Lenten one, which is at its best when made with the first tender vine leaves of the year, either picked from the vines growing in every Greek family garden or bought in the laiki – the street markets that thrive in Greek towns and cities. If fresh vine leaves are not available, look out for preserved ones in Greek grocers and some supermarkets.

**1** If using fresh leaves, blanch them briefly in batches in a pan of boiling water, lifting them out with a slotted spoon after a few seconds and draining them in a colander. They should just be wilted to make them pliable; not cooked. Preserved leaves can be extremely salty and must be rinsed well before being immersed in a bowl of hot water. Leave the vine leaves in the water for 4–5 minutes, then drain them, rinse them and drain them again.

**2** Put the rice in a large bowl and add the onions, spring onions, pine nuts, dill, mint and parsley. Mix well, then stir in half the olive oil and half the lemon juice. Season with salt and pepper and mix again.

**3** Line the bottom of a wide pan with 2–3 of the vine leaves. Spread another vine leaf out on a board veined side up and place a heaped teaspoon of the stuffing near the stalk end. Fold the two opposite sides of the leaf over the stuffing and then roll up tightly from the stalk end. Make more dolmathes in the same way and pack them tightly together in circles in the pan.

**4** Mix the remaining olive oil and lemon juice and pour the mixture over the dolmathes. Invert a small plate on top of the top layer to hold it down and prevent the rolls from unravelling. Carefully pour in the hot water, cover tightly and simmer gently for 1 hour. Serve the dolmathes hot or at room temperature. They look wonderful on a platter lined with fresh vine leaves, surrounded by the lemon wedges.

**Careful chopping is essential**
Don't be tempted to grate the onions, which would make them too moist. They can be either cut by hand into very tiny pieces or chopped coarsely in a food processor.

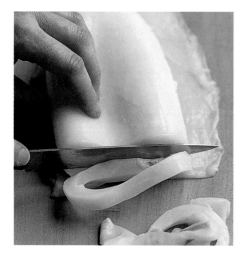

1kg/2¼lb fresh cuttlefish
150ml/¼ pint/⅔ cup extra virgin olive oil
1 large onion, about 225g/8oz, chopped
1 glass white wine, about 175ml/
    6fl oz/¾ cup
300ml/½ pint/1¼ cups hot water
500g/1¼lb potatoes, peeled and cubed
4–5 spring onions (scallions), chopped
juice of 1 lemon
60ml/4 tbsp chopped fresh dill
salt and ground black pepper

**Serves 4 as a main course
6 as a first course**

# cuttlefish with potatoes
soupies me patates

**Cuttlefish is sweeter and more tender than squid, provided you buy small or medium-size specimens. If the only ones available are very large, cook them for a little longer than stated in the recipe. This wonderful dish is often eaten during Lent.**

**1** Prepare the cuttlefish as for squid, following the instructions in the introduction to the Winter chapter. Rinse and drain them well, then slice them in 2cm/¾in wide ribbons.

**2** Heat the oil in a heavy pan, add the onion and sauté for about 5 minutes until light golden. Add the cuttlefish and sauté until all the water they exude has evaporated and the flesh starts to change colour. This will take 10–15 minutes.

**3** Pour in the wine and, when it has evaporated, add the water. Cover and cook for 10 minutes, then add the potatoes, spring onions, lemon juice, and salt and pepper. There should be enough water to almost cover the ingredients; top up if necessary. Cover and cook gently for 40 minutes or until the cuttlefish is tender, stirring occasionally. Add the dill and cook for 5 minutes. Serve hot.

1 onion, sliced
50g/2oz/¼ cup butter
60ml/4 tbsp extra virgin olive oil
2 large leeks, total weight about
    450g/1lb, chopped
115g/4oz/1 cup plain (all-purpose) flour
2.5ml/½ tsp bicarbonate of soda
    (baking soda)
3 large (US extra large) eggs, lightly beaten
200g/7oz Greek (strained plain) yogurt
300g/11oz feta cheese, cubed
115g/4oz/1–1⅓ cups freshly grated
    Gruyère or Parmesan cheese
45–60ml/3–4 tbsp chopped fresh dill
salt and ground black pepper

**Serves 4**

# electra's cheese and leek pie
electra's tyropitta

**This used to be a real treat whenever our
friend Electra invited us for drinks on the
island of Alonnisos. This pie is unusual by
Greek standards because it is not enclosed
in pastry. Serve tyropitta with the mezethes,
or as a lovely lunch, with a fresh green salad.**

**1** Sauté the onion in the butter and oil until light
golden. Add the leeks and cook over a low heat
for 10–12 minutes until soft. Cool a little.

**2** Preheat the oven to 180°C/350°F/Gas 4.
Lightly grease a 23cm/9in round springform
cake tin (pan). Sift the flour and bicarbonate of
soda into a bowl. Stir in the eggs, then the
yogurt and feta cheese, and finally the leek and
onion mixture. Set aside 30ml/2 tbsp of the
grated Gruyère or Parmesan and add the rest to
the batter, with the dill. Mix well and season.

**3** Spoon the mixture into the prepared tin and
level the surface. Sprinkle the reserved cheese
over the top and bake for 40–45 minutes until
golden. Let the pie cool before removing it from
the tin. Serve in wedges and offer some tasty
olive oil to be drizzled on top. Garnish with
lemon wedges, black olives and radishes.

675g/1½lb salt cod
800g/1¾lb potatoes, peeled and cut into
    small wedges
1 large onion, finely chopped
2–3 garlic cloves, chopped
leaves from 1 fresh rosemary sprig
30ml/2 tbsp chopped fresh flat
    leaf parsley
120ml/4fl oz/½ cup extra virgin olive oil
400g/14oz can chopped tomatoes
15ml/1 tbsp tomato purée (paste)
300ml/½ pint/1¼ cups hot water
5ml/1 tsp dried oregano
12 black olives
ground black pepper

**Serves 4 as a main course
6 as a first course**

# baked salt cod with potatoes, tomatoes and olives
## bakaliaros plaki sto fourno

Salt cod has been a winter staple in Greece for generations. It is particularly popular in the spring, and the following dish is often on the menu at city restaurants on Fridays during Lent. The dried, creamy-coloured sides of cod, sparkling with salt flakes, can often be seen in the central market in Athens and on the stalls in many street markets.

Although it is an acquired taste, salt cod does have an exotic aura about it and, if you get a plump piece of good quality fish, it can be very appetizing.

Served with plenty of thickly sliced fresh bread, this dish makes a main course for four or a dinner party first course for six. It can also be served cold, as part of the mezethes.

**1** Soak the cod in cold water overnight, changing the water as often as possible in the course of the evening and during the following day. The cod does not have to be skinned for this dish, but you should remove any obvious fins or bones.

**2** Preheat the oven to 180°C/350°F/Gas 4. Mix the potatoes, onion, garlic, rosemary and parsley in a large roasting pan. Grind in plenty of pepper. Add the olive oil and toss the mixture until well coated.

**3** Drain the cod and cut it into serving pieces. Arrange the pieces of cod between the coated vegetables and spread the tomatoes over the surface. Stir the tomato purée into the hot water until dissolved, then pour the mixture over the contents of the tin. Sprinkle the oregano on top. Bake for 1 hour, basting the fish and potatoes occasionally with the pan juices.

**4** Remove the roasting pan from the oven, sprinkle the olives on top, then cook it for 30 minutes more, adding a little more hot water if the mixture seems to be drying out. Garnish with fresh herbs. Serve hot or cold.

### Where to find salt cod
Salt cod can often be bought from Italian and Spanish groceries, as well as from Greek food stores. It is often sold in small squares, ready for soaking and draining. If you buy it in the piece, cut it into 7cm/2¾in squares after soaking.

1 glass red wine, about 175ml/
   6fl oz/¾ cup
60ml/4 tbsp red wine vinegar
1 rabbit, jointed
2 bay leaves, crushed
45ml/3 tbsp plain (all-purpose) flour
90–105ml/6–7 tbsp extra virgin olive oil
2 carrots, cut in thick batons, about
   10cm/4in in length
2 celery sticks, sliced
3 garlic cloves, halved lengthways
1 cinnamon stick
3–4 whole allspice
1–2 fresh rosemary sprigs
15ml/1 tbsp tomato purée (paste) diluted
   in 300ml/½ pint/1¼ cups water
675g/1½lb small, pickling-size
   onions, peeled
15ml/1 tbsp demerara (raw) sugar
salt and ground black pepper

**Serves 4**

# rabbit casserole with baby onions
kouneli stifatho

A good way to transform mild-tasting rabbit meat into an extremely appetizing dish. The multi-layered sweet and savoury flavours combine with the warm spices to permeate the meat. Serve the stifatho with a green salad to counterbalance its richness and add a note of freshness.

**1** Mix together the wine and vinegar in a shallow dish that is large enough to hold the rabbit joints in a single layer. Add the bay leaves and rabbit, turning to coat them in the mixture. Marinate for 4–6 hours, preferably overnight, turning the pieces over at least once.

**2** Lift the rabbit joints out of the marinade and pat them dry with kitchen paper. Reserve the marinade. Coat the pieces of rabbit lightly with the flour.

**3** Heat half of the oil in a large heavy frying pan and add the pieces of rabbit. Fry them, turning the pieces occasionally, until they are lightly browned on both sides, then place them in a flameproof casserole.

**4** Preheat the oven to 160°C/325°F/Gas 3. Add the carrots and celery to the oil remaining in the frying pan.

**5** Sauté the vegetables over a gentle heat for about 3 minutes. Add the garlic. As soon as it becomes aromatic, add the contents of the pan to the rabbit joints in the casserole.

**6** Place the casserole over a medium heat. Pour in the reserved marinade and let the wine bubble and evaporate. Add the spices, rosemary and the tomato purée mixture, cover and cook in the oven for 1 hour.

**7** Meanwhile, heat the remaining oil in the frying pan and add the small onions. They must be in a single layer, so fry them in batches if necessary. Fry them until they start to turn light golden, shaking the pan and turning them over occasionally. Sprinkle the demerara sugar over them, shake the pan, then let them brown and caramelize for 5–6 minutes more. Set aside.

**8** When the rabbit has cooked for an hour, spread the caramelized onions on top and add enough hot water to almost cover them. Cover the casserole, return it to the oven and cook for one more hour. Serve on warm plates, garnished with fresh rosemary.

75ml/5 tbsp extra virgin olive oil
1.6kg/3½lb organic or free-range
    chicken, jointed
1 large onion, roughly chopped
1 generous glass red wine, about
    250ml/8fl oz/1 cup
30ml/2 tbsp tomato purée (paste) diluted
    in 450ml/¾ pint/scant 2 cups hot water
1 cinnamon stick
3–4 whole allspice
2 bay leaves
salt and ground black pepper
boiled rice, orzo or fried potatoes, to serve

**Serves 4**

# spicy chicken casserole with red wine
kotopoulo kokkinisto alonnisou

This is the traditional chicken dish on Alonnisos. It is rather special, so tends to be reserved for Sundays and religious festivals. However, it is also often on the menu at Meltemi, our favourite restaurant on the beach of Megalo Mourtia. In Greece, it is usually served with plain rice or orzo, the small tear-shaped pasta, which is called kritharaki in Greek, but it is even better with home-made, thick, fried potatoes.

**1** Heat the oil in a large pan or sauté pan and brown the chicken pieces on both sides. Lift them out with tongs and set them aside.

**2** Add the onion to the hot oil and stir over a medium heat until it looks translucent.

**3** Return the chicken pieces to the pan, pour the wine over and cook for 2–3 minutes, until it has reduced. Add the tomato purée mixture, cinnamon, allspice and bay leaves. Season well with salt and pepper. Cover the pan and cook gently for 1 hour or until the chicken is tender. Serve with rice, orzo or fried potatoes.

75ml/5 tbsp extra virgin olive oil
4–6 thick shoulder of lamb steaks, with
  the bone in
1 large onion, thinly sliced
5–6 spring onions (scallions),
  roughly chopped
2 carrots, sliced in rounds
juice of 1 lemon
1.2kg/2½lb fresh peas in pods, shelled
  (this will give you about 500–675g/
  1¼–1½lb peas)
60ml/4 tbsp finely chopped fresh dill
salt and ground black pepper

**Serves 4–6**

# spring lamb casserole with fresh peas
arnaki me araka

In Greece, milk-fed lamb is at its best in April
and May, which is about the time when fresh
peas put in an appearance in the markets.
They are combined here to produce one of
the most delicious Greek dishes – a real treat.

**1** Heat the oil in a wide, heavy pan. Brown the
lamb on both sides. Lift out, then sauté the
onion slices in the oil remaining in the pan until
translucent. Add the spring onions and, 1 minute
later, the carrots. Sauté for 3–4 minutes.

**2** Return the lamb steaks to the pan, pour the
lemon juice over them and let it evaporate for
a few seconds. Pour over enough hot water to
cover the meat. Add salt and pepper. Cover and
simmer for 45–50 minutes, until the meat is
almost tender, turning the steaks over and
stirring the vegetables from time to time.

**3** Add the peas and half the dill, with a little more
water, if needed. Replace the lid and cook for
20–30 minutes until the meat and vegetables
are fully cooked. Sprinkle the remaining dill over
the casserole just before serving.

45ml/3 tbsp olive oil
1 onion, chopped
1kg/2¼lb boned leg of lamb, sliced in
 4–6 medium steaks
2 cos lettuces, coarsely shredded
6 spring onions (scallions), sliced
60ml/4 tbsp roughly chopped fresh dill,
 plus extra to garnish (optional)
2 eggs
15ml/1 tbsp cornflour (cornstarch) mixed
 to a paste with 120ml/4fl oz/½ cup water
juice of 1 lemon
salt

Serves 4–6

# lamb and cos lettuce casserole
arnaki fricassee

One of the classic Greek dishes, this is found on the islands and the mainland from the Ionian to the Aegean Sea. It is a favourite treat during the period following Easter, when young lambs are at their best and lettuces and fresh dill are to be found in abundance in open-air street markets.

It is an ideal choice for a dinner party, partly because it can be cooked in advance and carefully reheated, but more importantly because it is always a great success with its unusual flavours.

Make sure that the final dish has quite a lot of liquid as this will be transformed into the delicious avgolemono sauce. Serve it with plenty of fresh bread, to enjoy every last drop.

1 Heat the olive oil in a large, heavy pan. Add the chopped onion and sauté for 3–5 minutes, until it glistens and becomes translucent.

2 Increase the heat, then add the lamb steaks and cook, turning them over frequently, until all the moisture has been driven off, a process that will take about 15 minutes.

3 Add salt to taste and enough hot water to cover the meat. Cover the pan and simmer for about 1 hour, until the meat is only just tender.

4 Add the lettuces, spring onions and dill. If necessary, pour in a little more hot water so that all the vegetables are almost covered. Replace the lid on the pan and simmer for 15–20 minutes more. Remove from the heat and let the dish stand for 5 minutes while you prepare the ingredients for the sauce.

5 Beat the eggs lightly in a bowl, add the cornflour mixture and beat until smooth. Add the lemon juice and whisk briefly, then continue to whisk while gradually adding 75–90ml/5–6 tbsp of the hot liquid from the pan containing the lamb.

6 Pour the sauce over the meat. Do not stir; instead gently shake and rotate the pan until the sauce is incorporated with the remaining liquid. Return the pan to a gentle heat for 2–3 minutes, just long enough to warm the sauce through. Do not let it boil, or the sauce is likely to curdle. Serve on warmed plates and scatter over some extra chopped dill, if you like.

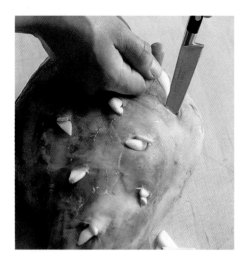

1 leg of lamb, about 2kg/4½lb
3 garlic cloves, quartered lengthways,
    plus 6–8 whole, unpeeled garlic cloves,
    or 1–2 heads of garlic, halved
900g/2lb potatoes, peeled and quartered
    lengthways
juice of 1 lemon
45ml/3 tbsp extra virgin olive oil
450ml/¾ pint/scant 2 cups hot water
5ml/1 tsp dried Greek oregano
2.5ml/½ tsp dried Greek thyme or 5ml/
    1 tsp chopped fresh thyme
salt and ground black pepper

**Serves 6–8**

# roast lamb with potatoes and garlic
arnaki sto fourno me patates

This is the Greek equivalent of the Sunday roast. There is a difference, though, in the way a Greek roast is cooked. In the old days, homes did not have ovens, so the food was sent to the local baker in the morning and collected at lunch time. It was essential to have everything in a single dish, so the meat and potatoes were arranged in a rather large aluminium container and sprinkled with olive oil and herbs before being taken to the baker. He would add water to keep the meat moist before cooking it in his fierce oven. The result was a complete meal, with meat, potatoes and gravy in one dish.

Roasts are mostly cooked at home nowadays (though some traditional village bakers maintain the tradition of cooking the villagers' Sunday lunches), but the method remains much the same.

**1** Preheat the oven to 220ºC/425ºF/Gas 7. Place the meat in a large roasting pan. Make several incisions in it and insert one or two sticks of garlic into each one.

**2** Arrange the potatoes and whole garlic cloves or halved heads of garlic around the meat, pour the lemon juice and olive oil over, and add half the water to the dish. Sprinkle over half the herbs, and some seasoning.

**3** Roast the lamb for 15 minutes, then reduce the oven temperature to 190ºC/375ºF/Gas 5. Roast for 1 hour. Turn the meat over so that the other side browns as well, sprinkle over the rest of the herbs and seasoning, and turn the potatoes over gently. Add the remaining hot water to the tin and cook for another 25–30 minutes, basting occasionally with the pan juices.

**4** Cover the meat with a clean dishtowel and let it rest for 10 minutes before serving. The cloves of garlic can be popped out of their skins and eaten with the meat; they will be deliciously creamy.

225g/8oz/2 cups plain (all-purpose) flour
    sifted with a pinch of salt
30ml/2 tbsp caster (superfine) sugar
115g/4oz/½ cup unsalted butter, cubed
45–60ml/3–4 tbsp cold water

**For the filling**
4 eggs
50g/2oz/¼ cup caster (superfine) sugar
15ml/1 tbsp plain (all-purpose) flour
500g/1¼lb/2½ cups fresh myzithra or
    ricotta cheese
60ml/4 tbsp Greek thyme-scented honey
2.5ml/½ tsp ground cinnamon

**Serves 6–8**

# sifnos cheese and honey tart
melopitta siffnou

This is a kind of Aegean cheesecake, made with honey and the fresh, unsalted local cheese called myzithra, which is similar to the Italian ricotta. Cakes like these are an Easter speciality in the Cyclades, particularly in Sifnos and Ios. Santorini has a similar speciality called militinia; small individual pastries filled with myzithra, eggs and sugar and flavoured with aromatic mastic resin. A similar and equally mouthwatering speciality in Crete is called lyhnarakia (little lanterns).

1 Mix the flour and sugar in a bowl, then rub in the butter until the mixture resembles breadcrumbs. Add the water, a little at a time, until the mixture clings together and forms a dough. It should not be too wet. Draw it into a ball, wrap it in clear film (plastic wrap) and chill for 30 minutes.

2 Preheat the oven to 180°C/350°F/Gas 4. Put a baking sheet in the oven to heat. Place the pastry on a lightly floured surface, roll out thinly and use to line a 25cm/10in round springform tin (pan). Carefully trim off any excess pastry.

3 Make the filling. Beat the eggs in a bowl, add the sugar and flour and beat until fluffy. Add the cheese, honey and half the cinnamon and beat until well mixed.

4 Pour the cheese mixture into the pastry case and level the surface. Place the tin on the hot baking sheet and cook the tart for 50–60 minutes, until light golden. Remove the tart from the oven and sprinkle with the remaining cinnamon while still hot.

**Time-saving pastry**
You could save time by using a 500g/1¼lb packet of ready-made fresh or thawed frozen shortcrust pastry instead of making your own.

# summer

sweet, ripe tomatoes, scented herbs
and plump, purple aubergines

### Summer is the most glorious of

seasons: the season of the Greek islands; of standing on island quays to watch fishing boats unload their catch; of living outdoors, even if that only means a small balcony in a block of flats in hot, noisy, cosmopolitan Athens.

Greek summers are defined for me firstly by the smell of jasmine and secondly by lunches under the silvery foliage of the olive trees by a dazzling white beach. The predominant memory is of sitting in our small garden in Athens as a child, and being engulfed in waves of exotic scent. The second image evokes the unmistakable tastes of summer on a small Greek island. We are enjoying a magnificent meal at "The Olive Grove" on the beach of Lefto Yialo on Alonnisos. Marvellous dishes glide out of Magda Anagnostou's kitchen: richly flavoured baked aubergines (eggplant) accompanied by bowls of cooling tzatziki; octopus with pasta; baked fish plaki and, of course, the crowning glory of summer food – the grilled slices of glistening, opaque swordfish or mayatico, a kind of white-fleshed tuna. There are dark slices of tuna, too, and the alabaster bodies of whole squid stuffed with crumbly, salty feta cheese.

When dusk descends, it is time for barbecues, and the very best of these were cooked by Panagiotis Kaloyiannis or Nikos

Malamatenios in the Old Village on Alonnisos. This is the time for grilled souvlaki – tender cubes of pork or lamb immersed in garlic marinades, then skewered and cooked over the coals. Chicken souvlaki is equally tasty, especially when served with the tapered green peppers that are typical of the island, and sprinkled with aromatic oregano before being grilled. Most delicious of all, perhaps, are the plump, white cubes of swordfish souvlaki.

Summer injects a joyful and playful character into the Greek kitchen. Colourful vegetables acquire a special importance, particularly on the lunch table. Simple lunches, such as strapatsatha – fresh tomatoes cooked with scrambled eggs – acquire an incomparable flavour as they blend the heat of the sun with the sweetness of summer. This is the season

**Left**
Summer is the season of regal, purple aubergines, which are cooked in myriad ways: slow-cooked in sauces, baked with stuffings, or sliced and fried for the classic Greek moussaka.

**Above**
Thyme is indigenous to Greece and grows wild on the hillsides. It is picked throughout the summer and then dried in bunches to be used to flavour dishes during the winter months.

of the regal, purple aubergine, which can transform the most ordinary vegetable dish into a veritable feast.

Anyone who visits Greece in summer should plan a visit to a local baker at lunchtime to smell the magnificent aroma of whatever is being cooked that day. Traditionally, Greek homes did not have ovens, so meals were prepared in large, round aluminium containers called tapsia, which were taken to the local baker in the morning to be baked in ovens that were still hot after the day's bread-making. This practical solution had another advantage, too, in that it ensured that while the bakery grew hot, the village houses stayed cool. Even today, when almost every home possesses an electric oven, on extremely hot summer days it is still possible to witness the parade of the tapsia along streets and paths to the local baker.

Summer brings one of the most important religious days in the Greek Orthodox Church – Assumption, on 15 August, which commemorates the ascension of the Virgin Mary into heaven. A glittering occasion on the Greek islands, it is preceded by two weeks of fasting. The day itself is celebrated with a string of festivities. After attending the morning liturgy, most people will sit down to a special lunch. On the table will be roast lamb with potatoes and garlic, roast kid or the mouthwatering yiouvetsi (baked lamb with tomatoes, garlic and pasta).

After the long days of fasting, everyone will eat well – and why not? Summer is, after all, the season of excess. Indulgence is the order of the day. Colourful vegetables and richly scented fresh herbs – these are the ingredients that make summer dishes such as barbecued souvlaki so special.

**Top**
In a traditional Greek kitchen, wonderfully plump and irregularly shaped, sun-ripened tomatoes are washed ready for a stew or casserole.

**Bottom**
Fishing boats at dusk, tied at the quay in Hydra harbour. One of the delights of a Greek summer is to stand on an island quay and watch the fishermen unload their catch.

**Far left**
Plump, purple aubergines are one of the Greek's most popular summer vegetables and are cooked in a host of dishes.

**Left**
Another favourite Greek vegetable, okra is cooked in slowly simmered casseroles with tomatoes, meat or poultry.

**In Greek summer cooking**, without a doubt, the protagonists are vegetables. From unevenly shaped, sugary tomatoes to regal aubergines, and from exotic okra to the various varieties of fresh green beans, they constitute the light character of Greek cuisine in summer.

### Aubergines

Plump aubergines (eggplant) are among the favourite summer vegetables in Greece and are made into many different dishes. In the past, they were inclined to be bitter, so it was necessary to slice and soak them in salted water before cooking. Fortunately, this is seldom necessary with modern varieties, although it is still recommended in some recipes. Aubergines love oil, and soak it up like blotting paper, so must be cooked with care. Baking can be a healthier cooking method than frying.

### Okra

The green pods of a tall annual, okra is also known by the descriptive name of lady's fingers. The parent plant can reach a height of 2m (6ft). In Greece, okra pods tend to be quite small and slim, but elsewhere they do vary in size. They have to be handled gently, so that they do not get bruised.

The vegetable originated in Africa and is widely used in Creole cooking. Okra's main claim to fame is that, when sliced, it oozes a

sticky liquid, which acts as a thickener when the pods are cooked. When the pods are cooked whole, they have a sweet taste and a melting texture. Okra is a real favourite in Greece. It tastes delicious with both meat or chicken, but is more often often cooked in bamies, a casserole with fresh tomatoes, which is one of my favourite lunches, especially when served with chunks of feta cheese and slices of crusty bread.

### Preparing okra

• When preparing okra for cooking whole, pare off the conical head from each pod, using a small sharp knife, either making a straight cut or angling the knife slightly.

• Take care not to cut so deep that you expose the seeds inside.
• Remove the black tip at the other end, again taking care not to cut too deeply.
• Rinse the pods quickly under cold water and drain them well. Don't slice the pods unless you need the mucilaginous liquid to thicken the dish.

**Left**
In Greece, fine green beans are often boiled, dressed with olive oil and lemon juice and served as a salad.

**Below**
Purslane grows wild all over Greece. This delicate herb-like plant has a mild, refreshing lemony flavour.

to appear. These are the equivalent of fresh Italian borlotti beans and are always shelled before being cooked in casseroles.

## Purslane

This fleshy, herb-like plant is very prolific and grows like a weed all over Greece. The more you harvest the plant, the more it sprouts. Wild purslane is more slender and has smaller and crunchier leaves than the cultivated variety, which has silvery, furry leaves and thick, cacti-like stems. Both the leaves and thinner stems are used in salads. The plant has a light, lemony taste that is quite mild and refreshing. To prepare it, trim off any thick stems, then chop the leaves and remaining stems roughly. Dress it with olive oil and lemon juice. Purslane can also be combined with diced cucumber and tomatoes or other greens in a salad.

## Tomatoes

Although not a native of the Mediterranean, but a visitor brought over from America in the 16th century by Columbus, the tomato is firmly embedded in the Greek kitchen, and the cuisine would be much poorer in the summer without them as they couple so perfectly with other vegetables. Tomatoes are used in many ways. They can be stuffed or added to casseroles, and tomato salads in various combinations are ubiquitous. There are even delicious tomato rissoles made on the Aegean island of Santorini.

## Courgettes

Greek courgettes (zucchini) are different from the familiar dark green variety. They are pale, almost striped with white, smooth-skinned, and may be short and rounded. They have a sweet taste and are often fried, boiled and served as a salad, or stuffed. However, briami, courgettes baked with potatoes, remains my favourite.

## Fresh beans

The Greeks have several favourite green bean varieties. At the beginning of summer, the thin long ambellofasoula are boiled and served as a salad with olive oil and lemon. Then come tsaoulia, which resemble bobby beans, but the best and most delicious, are the flat barbounia. Around August, the scarlet-lined pods of handres – a lovely name meaning beads – start

### Capers

These grow wild in Greece. They are the immature flower buds of a pretty bush, which often appears to be trailing. If allowed to develop, the buds open into large pink flowers that resemble those of a wild rose. Capers are not eaten fresh, but are either pickled in brine or dry salted. On the Aegean island of Santorini, where they are especially proud of their capers, the islanders also pickle the young shoots of the caper bush, and serve them with olive oil as a special meze called kaparofylla, which is delicious. Rinse capers thoroughly before using them in a dish.

### Oregano

Known in Greece as rigani, this is the herb most closely identified with Greek cooking. A native of the Mediterranean, it is a small, woody plant with tiny green, unmistakably aromatic leaves. In Greece, oregano grows wild on hillsides and in fallow fields and, around the middle of July, it is a mass of small white flowers. Towards the end of that month, Greeks gather huge bunches of rigani, that they hang in a shady place for a week to dry. The aroma seems to intensify when the herb is dried, and the tops and leaves are crumbled and stored in jars for the dark winter months. Oregano is used constantly in the

Greek kitchen, and lends its distinctive flavour to a wide range of dishes, from bean soups and casseroles to souvlakia and fried meat balls.

### Thyme

Thymari, to give it its Greek name, is a small woody herb with purple flowers. It is indigenous to Greece and grows wild all over the hillsides. The aroma is superb and intensifies when the herb is dried. Like oregano, it is collected in bunches, then dried and stored for the winter months. It is an essential ingredient for roasts and grills of either fish or meat, and always seems to partner oregano – a marriage that is made in heaven.

**Left**
Oregano is synonomous with Greek cooking. This distinctive herb is used to flavour a wide range of dishes from grilled meats to soups and casseroles.

**Above**
Thyme – along with oregano – is an essential summer ingredient, often used to add flavour to skewered meats and fish that are cooked outdoors on a barbecue.

**Opposite**
Images of summer in Greece: clockwise front top left, bright yellow courgette (zucchini) flowers; chicken grilling on a barbecue with peppers and tomatoes; purslane leaves with cubes of feta, tomatoes, onions and olives ready for a summer salad; sun-ripened tomatoes still on the vine; and large Mediterranean prawns (shrimp) ready for grilling.

3 courgettes (zucchini)
1 aubergine (eggplant)
25g/1oz/¼ cup plain (all-purpose) flour
sunflower oil, for frying
salt and ground black pepper

**For the tzatziki**
15cm/6in piece of cucumber
1–2 garlic cloves, crushed
200g/7oz Greek (strained plain) yogurt
15ml/1 tbsp extra virgin olive oil
30ml/2 tbsp thinly sliced fresh
  mint leaves

**Serves 4**

# fried courgettes and aubergines with cucumber and yogurt dip
kolokythakia ke melitzanes me tzatziki

**Tzatziki is a simple but very refreshing appetizer that is well suited to the heat of the summer. It can be served with grilled meats and roasts, but its proper place, and the place where I think it works best of all, is with freshly fried slices of courgettes and aubergines. When served with a salad, this dish makes the perfect first course for a dinner or a light summer lunch.**

**1** Start by making the tzatziki. Peel the cucumber, grate it coarsely into a colander, then press out most of the liquid. Add the cucumber to the yogurt with the garlic, olive oil and mint. Stir in salt to taste, cover and chill.

**2** Trim the courgettes and aubergine, then rinse them and pat them dry. Cut them lengthways into thin, long slices and coat them lightly with the flour.

**3** Heat the oil in a large, heavy or non-stick frying pan and add as many courgette slices as the pan will hold in one layer. Cook for 1–2 minutes, until light golden, then turn them over and brown the other side. Lift the slices out, drain them on kitchen paper and keep them hot while cooking the remaining courgettes and then the aubergines.

**4** Pile the fried slices in a large warmed bowl, sprinkle with salt and pepper and serve immediately with the bowl of chilled tzatziki garnished with mint leaves.

**Hold the salt**
If you are making the tzatziki several hours before serving, don't add the salt until later. If salt is added too far in advance, it will make the yogurt watery.

3 large aubergines (eggplant), total weight
   about 900g/2lb
15ml/1 tbsp roughly chopped onion
2 garlic cloves, crushed
juice of ½ lemon, or a little more
90–105ml/6–7 tbsp extra virgin olive oil
1 ripe tomato, peeled, seeded
   and finely diced
salt and ground black pepper
finely chopped fresh flat leaf parsley,
   to garnish
chicory (Belgian endive) and black and
   green olives, to serve

**Serves 4**

# salad of puréed aubergines
melitzanosalata

In the heat of high summer, melitzanosalata
makes a surprisingly refreshing meze. To be
strictly authentic, the aubergines should be
grilled over charcoal, when they will have an
enticing, smoky aroma. The mixture is usually
served with toast or pitta bread.

**1** Prick the aubergines and grill them on a
barbecue over a low to medium heat for at least
1 hour, turning occasionally, until they are soft.
If you are cooking the aubergines in a domestic
oven, prick them and lay them directly on the
shelves. Roast at 180°C/350°F/Gas 4 for 1 hour,
or until soft. Turn them over twice.

**2** When the aubergines are cool enough to
handle, cut them in half. Spoon the flesh into a
food processor and add the onion, garlic and
lemon juice. Season and process until smooth.

**3** With the motor running, drizzle in the olive oil
through the feeder tube, until the mixture forms
a smooth paste. Taste the mixture and adjust
the seasoning, then spoon the mixture into a
bowl and stir in the diced tomato. Cover and
chill lightly. Garnish with parsley and serve with
chicory leaves and bowls of olives.

60ml/4 tbsp extra virgin olive oil
2–3 shallots, finely chopped
675g/1½lb sweet tomatoes,
    roughly chopped
pinch of dried oregano or 5ml/1 tsp
    chopped fresh thyme
2.5ml/½ tsp sugar
6 eggs, lightly beaten
salt and ground black pepper

**Serves 4**

# scrambled eggs with tomatoes
strapatsatha

Although this is a simple dish, it is positively
mouthwatering when made in the heart of
the summer with sweet, ripe tomatoes
picked straight from the garden or bought
from the local market.

Dishes like this are found all over the
Mediterranean, with regional variations.
For instance, French pipérade is similar, but
includes Bayonne ham.

Strapatsatha makes a delicious light lunch
on a sunny day. All you need add is a salad
and slices of crisp toast or fresh bread.

**1** Heat the olive oil in a large frying pan and
sauté the shallots, stirring occasionally, until
they are glistening and translucent.

**2** Stir in the tomatoes, herbs and sugar, with
salt and pepper to taste. Cook over a low heat
for about 15 minutes until most of the liquid has
evaporated and the sauce is thick.

**3** Add the beaten eggs to the pan and cook for
2–3 minutes, stirring continuously with a wooden
spatula as when making scrambled eggs. The
eggs should be just set, but not overcooked.
Serve immediately, garnished with fresh herbs.

3 medium aubergines (eggplant), total
   weight about 800g/1¾lb
150ml/¼ pint/⅔ cup extra virgin olive oil
2 large onions, finely chopped
3 garlic cloves, finely chopped
500g/1¼lb fresh tomatoes, peeled if you
   like, and chopped
2.5ml/½ tsp each dried oregano
   and thyme
2.5ml/½ tsp sugar
45ml/3 tbsp chopped fresh parsley
15ml/1 tbsp tomato purée (paste) diluted
   in 150ml/¼ pint/⅔ cup hot water
salt and ground black pepper

**Serves 4**

# aubergines with tomato topping
melitzanes imam bayildi

**Imam bayildi is perhaps the most famous Greek dish. These days, I make a lighter, easier version using slices of aubergine topped with the rich tomato, herb and olive oil stuffing. It can be served hot or left to cool slightly and served at room temperature, either accompanied by a salad as a main course or as part of the mezethes.**

**1** Trim the aubergines, then slice them into rounds, about 1cm/½in thick. Heat half the olive oil in a large frying pan and shallow-fry the aubergines in batches, turning them over once, until light golden on both sides. As each batch is cooked, lift the slices out and arrange them side by side in a large roasting dish.

**2** Heat the rest of the oil in a saucepan and sauté the onions until lightly coloured. Add the garlic and when aromatic, add the tomatoes and a little water. Season, stir in the oregano, thyme and sugar, then cover and cook for 15 minutes, stirring occasionally.

**3** Preheat the oven to 190°C/375°F/Gas 5. Stir the parsley into the sauce, then pile 15–30ml/1–2 tbsp of the mixture on each slice of aubergine. Pour the diluted tomato purée into the dish, adding it to a corner, to avoid disturbing the aubergines. Bake the aubergines for 20–25 minutes, basting them once.

**4** Serve hot or at room temperature, either accompanied by a salad as a main course or as part of the mezethes for a party.

4 large aubergines (eggplant), total weight
  about 1.2kg/2½lb
150ml/¼ pint/⅔ cup sunflower oil
50g/2oz/½ cup freshly grated Parmesan
  or Cheddar cheese

**For the sauce**
45ml/3 tbsp extra virgin olive oil
2 garlic cloves, crushed
2 x 400g/14oz cans tomatoes
5ml/1 tsp tomato purée (paste)
2.5ml/½ tsp sugar
2.5ml/½ tsp dried Greek oregano
30–45ml/2–3 tbsp chopped fresh flat
  leaf parsley
salt and ground black pepper

**Serves 4**

# aubergines baked with tomatoes and cheese
melitzanes sto fourno

**This is a delectable dish, particularly when made in the middle of summer when the aubergines are at their sweetest.**

**1** Trim the aubergines and cut lengthways into 1cm/½in thick slices. Heat the oil in a large frying pan and fry the slices briefly in batches. Lift out as soon as they are golden on both sides and drain on kitchen paper.

**2** Arrange the aubergine slices in two layers in a baking dish. Sprinkle with salt and pepper.

**3** Make the sauce. Heat the oil gently in a large pan, add the garlic and sauté for a few seconds, then add the tomatoes, tomato purée, sugar and oregano and season to taste. Cover and simmer for 25–30 minutes or until the sauce is thick and velvety, stirring occasionally. Stir in the parsley and cook for 2–3 minutes.

**4** Meanwhile, preheat the oven to 180ºC/350ºF/ Gas 4. Spread the sauce over the aubergines to cover them. Sprinkle the cheese on top and bake for 40 minutes.

675g/1½lb fresh okra
150ml/¼ pint/⅔ cup extra virgin olive oil
1 large onion, sliced
675g/1½lb fresh tomatoes, sliced, or
   400g/14oz can chopped tomatoes
2.5ml/½ tsp sugar
30ml/2 tbsp finely chopped flat
   leaf parsley
salt and ground black pepper

**Serves 4 as a main course
6 as a first course**

# slow-cooked okra casserole with tomatoes
bamies

Okra makes a deliciously sweet casserole and, as far as vegetarian dishes go, this is one of the best. Made with fresh tomatoes, at the height of the summer, it is certainly my favourite lunch, especially when served with a fresh-tasting feta cheese and crusty bread. It can be served hot or at room temperature.

**1** Prepare the okra pods as described in the introduction to this chapter.

**2** Heat the oil in a large deep pan or sauté pan and fry the onion slices until light golden. Stir in the fresh or canned tomatoes, with the sugar and salt and pepper to taste. Cook for 5 minutes.

**3** Add the okra and shake the pan to distribute them evenly and coat them in the sauce. The okra should be immersed in the sauce, so add a little hot water if necessary.

**4** Cook gently for 30–40 minutes, depending on the size of the okra. Shake the pan occasionally, but do not stir. Add the parsley just before serving.

800g/1¾lb green beans, trimmed
150ml/¼ pint/⅔ cup extra virgin olive oil
1 large onion, thinly sliced
2 garlic cloves, chopped
2 small potatoes, peeled and cubed
675g/1½lb tomatoes or a 400g/14oz can
    plum tomatoes, chopped
150ml/¼ pint/⅔ cup hot water
45–60ml/3–4 tbsp chopped fresh parsley
salt and ground black pepper

**Serves 4**

# fresh green beans with tomato sauce
fasolakia

This is one of the standard summer dishes in Greece and is made with different kinds of fresh beans according to what is available. When the beans are tender and the tomatoes sweet, the dish, although frugal, can have an astoundingly good flavour. It is usually accompanied by feta cheese and fresh bread.

**1** If the beans are very long, cut them in half. Drop them into a bowl of cold water.

**2** Heat the olive oil in a large pan, add the onion and sauté until translucent. Add the garlic, then, when it becomes aromatic, stir in the potatoes and sauté the mixture for a few minutes.

**3** Add the tomatoes, with the hot water and cook for 5 minutes. Drain the beans, rinse them and drain again, then add them to the pan with a little salt and pepper to season. Cover and simmer for 30 minutes. Stir in the chopped parsley, with a little more hot water if the mixture looks dry. Cook for 10 minutes more, until the beans are very tender. Serve hot with slices of feta cheese, if you like.

225g/8oz tomatoes
1 red onion, thinly sliced
1 green (bell) pepper, cored and sliced in
  thin ribbons
1 piece of cucumber, about 15cm/6in
  in length, peeled and sliced in rounds
150g/5oz feta cheese, cubed
a large handful of fresh purslane,
  trimmed of thick stalks and rinsed
8–10 black olives
90–105ml/6–7 tbsp extra virgin olive oil
15ml/1 tbsp lemon juice
1.5ml/¼ tsp dried oregano
salt and ground black pepper

**Serves 4**

# sun-ripened tomato and feta salad with purslane

horiatiki salata me glystritha

Horiatiki salad is the summer staple of tourists. They know it simply as Greek salad and relish it for its combination of tomato, pepper, onion, cucumber, feta and olives. Locals often prefer this more unusual version, made with the crunchy addition of fresh purslane that grows wild in gardens and uncultivated fields. It is the ideal accompaniment to grilled fish or squid and grilled meats but, as it is quite a substantial affair, it could make a light summer lunch by itself when accompanied with fresh crusty bread. A good alternative to purslane is rocket (arugula).

**1** Cut the tomatoes in quarters and place them in a salad bowl. Add the onion, green pepper, cucumber, feta, purslane and olives.

**2** Sprinkle the olive oil, lemon juice and oregano on top. Add salt and pepper to taste, then toss to coat everything in the lovely olive oil and lemon and amalgamate the flavours. If possible, let the salad stand for 10–15 minutes at room temperature before serving.

4 cod or hake steaks
2–3 fresh flat leaf parsley sprigs
4 slices white bread, toasted, then
   crumbed in a food processor

**For the sauce**
75–90ml/5–6 tbsp extra virgin olive oil
1 glass white wine, 175ml/6fl oz/¾ cup
2 garlic cloves, crushed
60ml/4 tbsp finely chopped flat
   leaf parsley
1 fresh red or green chilli, seeded and
   finely chopped
400g/14oz ripe tomatoes, peeled and
   finely diced
salt and ground black pepper

**Serves 4**

# baked fish in the style of spetse
## psari a la spetsiota

**All kinds of fish are prepared in this way on the tiny island of Spetse. Serve with a large fresh salad, or with little boiled potatoes and garlicky green beans, for a summer meal.**

**1** Mix all the sauce ingredients in a bowl and add some salt and pepper. Set the mixture aside.

**2** Preheat the oven to 190°C/375°F/Gas 5. Rinse the fish steaks and pat them dry. Place the steaks in a single layer in an oiled baking dish and scatter over the parsley. Season with salt and pepper.

**3** Spoon the sauce over the fish, then sprinkle over half the breadcrumbs. Bake for 10 minutes, then baste with the juices in the dish. Sprinkle the remaining breadcrumbs over, then bake for a further 10–15 minutes.

### Try whole fish cooked this way
Use two fish, such as sea bass or grey mullet, total weight about 1kg/2¼lb. Rinse thoroughly, inside and out, pat dry, then tuck the parsley sprigs inside. Add the sauce and breadcumbs as above. Bake for 15 minutes, then turn both fish over carefully, and bake for 20–25 minutes.

75ml/5 tbsp extra virgin olive oil
1 onion, chopped
½ red (bell) pepper, seeded
   and cubed
675g/1½lb ripe tomatoes, peeled and
   roughly chopped
generous pinch of sugar
2.5ml/½ tsp dried oregano
450g/1lb peeled (but with the tail shells
   intact) raw tiger or king prawns (jumbo
   shrimp), thawed if frozen
30ml/2 tbsp finely chopped fresh flat
   leaf parsley
75g/3oz feta cheese, cubed
salt and ground black pepper

**Serves 4**

# prawns with tomatoes and feta
garithes yiouvetsi

This luxurious and unusual dish takes its
name from the container in which it is
traditionally cooked. A yiouvetsi is a round
baking dish without a lid. It is made from
glazed, dark red earthenware.

   For me, this particular prawn dish always
conjures up memories of sunny lunches by
the sea. Serve it as a first course for six,
with plenty of crusty bread for mopping up
the sauce, or with rice as a main course.

**1** Heat the oil in a frying pan, add the onion and
sauté gently for a few minutes until translucent.
Add the cubed red pepper and cook, stirring
occasionally, for 2–3 minutes more.

**2** Stir in the chopped tomatoes, sugar and
oregano, then season with salt and pepper to
taste. Cook gently over a low heat for about
15 minutes, stirring occasionally, until the sauce
reduces slightly and thickens.

**3** Preheat the oven to 180°C/350°F/Gas 4. Stir
the prawns and parsley into the tomato sauce,
tip it into a baking dish and spread evenly.
Sprinkle the cheese cubes on top, then bake for
30 minutes. Serve hot with a fresh green salad.

2 red onions, quartered
2 red or green (bell) peppers, quartered
 and seeded
20–24 thick cubes of swordfish, prepared
 weight 675–800g/1½–1¾lb
75ml/5 tbsp extra virgin olive oil
1 garlic clove, crushed
large pinch of dried oregano
salt and ground black pepper

**Serves 4**

# grilled swordfish skewers
xifias souvlaki

Seeing a swordfish landed from a fishing boat in the main harbour on Alonnisos or in the little fishing village of Steni Vala is always a very exhilarating sight. What is even more exciting is the knowledge that soon there will be swordfish for sale at the small fish market close by, and that souvlaki will be on the menu that night.

Souvlakia are chunks of fish or meat that are threaded on long metal skewers, often with pieces of pepper and onions. The word is derived from souvla, the long metal spit that is inserted into a whole lamb or goat in order to spit-roast it over an open fire.

Both meat and fish souvlakia are at their best when grilled over an open fire. They acquire an unmistakable smoky aroma that makes their flavour even more tantalizing.

**1** Carefully separate the onion quarters in pieces, each composed of two or three layers. Slice each pepper quarter in half widthways.

**2** Make the souvlakia by threading five or six pieces of swordfish on to each of four long metal skewers, alternating with pieces of the pepper and onion. Lay the souvlakia across a grill pan or roasting tray and set aside while you make the basting sauce.

**3** Whisk the olive oil, garlic and oregano in a bowl. Add salt and pepper and whisk again. Brush the souvlakia generously on all sides with the basting sauce.

**4** Preheat the grill (broiler) to the highest setting or prepare a barbecue. Slide the grill pan or roasting tray underneath the grill or transfer the skewers to the barbecue, making sure that they are not too close to the heat. Cook for 8–10 minutes, turning the skewers several times, until the fish is cooked and the peppers and onions have begun to scorch around the edges. Every time you turn the skewers, brush them with the basting sauce.

**5** Serve the souvlakia immediately, with a cucumber, onion and olive salad.

### Cutting the fish
The fishmonger will prepare the cubes of swordfish for you, but if you prefer to do this yourself you will need 800g/1¾lb swordfish. The cubes should be fairly big – about 5cm/2in square.

4 medium squid, total weight
   about 900g/2lb
4–8 finger-length slices of feta cheese
90ml/6 tbsp olive oil
2 garlic cloves, crushed
3–4 fresh marjoram sprigs, leaves
   removed and chopped
salt and ground black pepper
lemon wedges, to serve

**Serves 4**

# grilled squid stuffed with feta cheese
## kalamarakia sharas me feta

Every summer, when we return to the island of Alonnisos, one of our first ports of call is the Olive Grove, Magda Anagnostou's lovely restaurant on the dazzling beach of Lefto Yialo. One of our favourite dishes is her grilled squid stuffed with feta cheese. The squid, by the way, is always caught the night before by Magda's father-in-law, unless the moon is full when the wily squid hide in the weeds.

A large, fresh leafy salad or a vegetable dish, such as fresh green beans with tomato sauce or slow-cooked okra casserole with tomatoes, could be served with the squid.

**1** Prepare the squid, following the instructions in the introduction to the Winter chapter, but keep the bodies intact. Rinse them thoroughly, inside and out, and drain well. Lay the squid bodies and tentacles in a shallow dish that will hold them in a single layer. Tuck the pieces of cheese between the squid.

**2** To make the marinade, pour the oil into a jug (pitcher) or bowl and whisk in the garlic and marjoram. Season to taste with salt and pepper. Pour the marinade over the squid and the cheese, then cover and leave in a cool place to marinate for 2–3 hours, turning once.

**3** Insert 1 or 2 pieces of cheese and a few bits of marjoram from the marinade in each squid and place them in a lightly oiled grill (broiler) pan or tray. Thread the tentacles on skewers.

**4** Preheat the grill to a fairly low setting or prepare a barbecue. Grill the stuffed squid gently for about 6 minutes, then turn them over carefully. Grill them for 1–2 minutes more, then add the skewered tentacles. Grill them for 2 minutes on each side, until they start to scorch. Serve the stuffed squid with the tentacles. Add a few lemon wedges, for squeezing over the seafood.

1.6kg/3½lb organic or free-range
  roasting chicken
90ml/6 tbsp extra virgin olive oil
5ml/1 tsp dried oregano
400g/14oz can plum tomatoes,
  roughly chopped
2 garlic cloves, chopped
450ml/¾ pint/scant 2 cups hot water
600g/1lb 6oz okra
45ml/3 tbsp chopped fresh flat
  leaf parsley
salt and ground black pepper

**Serves 4**

# baked chicken with okra
kotopoulo me bamies fournou

**My English husband became so enamoured of this dish when he first ate it at my parents' house in Athens in the early seventies, that from there on my mother used to include it in her menu whenever we stayed with them.**

**Okra – or lady's fingers as they are also known – are quite exotic in the West, but in Greece this vegetable is a summer staple. It is cooked on its own, can be combined with lamb or beef, and tastes delicious in a chicken casserole.**

**1** Preheat the oven to 200°C/400°F/Gas 6. Place the chicken breast down in a large roasting dish. Drizzle half the olive oil over it and sprinkle over half the dried oregano. Add the tomatoes, garlic and 300ml/½ pint/1¼ cups of the hot water to the dish. Transfer to the oven and bake for 30 minutes.

**2** Meanwhile, prepare the okra. Leave each okra pod whole and use a small sharp knife to peel the conical end. Be careful not to nick the pod and release the mucilaginous juices (see the introduction to this chapter for more information on preparing okra). You will soon get to grips with this task, but it is a good idea to get someone to help you. Rinse the okra thoroughly in cold water and then drain them well. Repeat until the water appears clear.

**3** After 30 minutes, remove the dish from the oven and turn the chicken over. Add the okra, spreading it evenly around the bird. Drizzle the remaining oil over, then sprinkle with the rest of the oregano. Season and add the parsley and the remaining hot water. Turn the okra with a spatula to coat it in the tomato sauce.

**4** Reduce the oven temperature to 190°C/375°F/Gas 5 and bake the chicken for 1 hour more, or until it is fully cooked and the okra is tender. Take the dish out of the oven occasionally and baste both the chicken and the okra.

**5** This dish is best served hot, but will happily wait for 30 minutes. It makes the perfect main course when accompanied by a salad and fresh bread.

**Checking the cooking time**
If you buy a larger chicken, or use large okra pods, you may need to increase the baking time. The chicken will be cooked when the joints move freely and the juices that flow, when the thickest part of the thigh is pierced with a knife, are no longer pink.

1½ chickens, total weight about
  2.25kg/5lb, jointed, or 12 chicken pieces
2–3 red or green (bell) peppers, quartered,
  and seeded
4–5 tomatoes, halved horizontally
lemon wedges, to serve

**For the marinade**
90ml/6 tbsp extra virgin olive oil
juice of 1 large lemon
5ml/1 tsp French mustard
4 garlic cloves, crushed
2 fresh red or green chillies, seeded
  and chopped
5ml/1 tsp dried oregano
salt and ground black pepper

**Serves 4–6**

# chargrilled chicken with garlic and peppers

kotopoulo sti shara me piperies

An imaginative marinade can make all the difference to the rather bland flavour of chicken. We often have this easy but delectable dish for dinner in the summer, as it is very pleasant to do the cooking under the stars rather than in a hot kitchen. All we have to do is to marinate the chicken and place it in the refrigerator before going to the beach in the morning. That evening, while the chicken is being cooked on the barbecue, we prepare a large salad and a bowl of tzatziki. You will find that, because the chicken is so mouthwatering, it is essential to make plenty of it. It always gets eaten.

**1** If you are jointing the chicken yourself, divide the legs into two. Make a couple of slits in the deepest part of the flesh of each piece of chicken, using a small sharp knife. This will help the marinade to be absorbed more efficiently and let the chicken cook thoroughly.

**2** Beat together all the marinade ingredients in a large bowl. Add the chicken pieces and turn them over to coat them thoroughly in the marinade. Cover the bowl with clear film (plastic wrap) and place in the refrigerator for 4–8 hours, turning the chicken pieces over in the marinade a couple of times, if possible.

**3** Prepare the barbecue. When the coals are ready, lift the chicken pieces out of the marinade and place them on the grill. Add the pepper pieces and the tomatoes to the marinade and set it aside for 15 minutes. Grill the chicken pieces for 20–25 minutes. Watch them closely and move them away from the area where the heat is most fierce if they start to burn.

**4** Turn the chicken pieces over and cook them for 20–25 minutes more. Meanwhile, thread the peppers on two long metal skewers. Add them to the barbecue grill, with the tomatoes, for the last 15 minutes of cooking. Remember to keep an eye on them and turn them over at least once. Serve with the lemon wedges.

### Cooking indoors
You can, of course, cook these under the grill (broiler). Have the heat fairly high, but don't place the pieces of chicken too close. They will probably need less time than when cooked over the coals – allow about 15 minutes each side.

675g/1½lb thin veal escalopes
  (veal scallops)
40g/1½oz/⅓ cup plain (all-purpose) flour
90ml/6 tbsp extra virgin olive oil
1 small onion, thinly sliced
3 garlic cloves, finely chopped
2–3 fresh sage leaves, finely chopped
1 glass white wine (175ml/6fl oz/¾ cup)
juice of ½ lemon
450ml/¾ pint/scant 2 cups beef or
  chicken stock
30ml/2 tbsp finely chopped fresh flat
  leaf parsley
salt and ground black pepper

**Serves 4**

# veal escalopes from corfu
sofrito

This is a favourite dinner party dish on the island of Corfu. It is clearly derived from the island's Venetian past as it was not known elsewhere in Greece until recently, when a cookery competition on Greek television brought it into the national limelight. Serve the sofrito with mashed potato or boiled new potatoes and a salad.

**1** Sprinkle the veal escalopes with a little salt and pepper, then coat them lightly in the flour.

**2** Heat the olive oil in a large frying pan over a medium heat. Add the escalopes and brown them lightly on both sides. Take the escalopes out and put them in a wide flameproof casserole.

**3** Add the onion to the oil remaining in the frying pan and sauté the slices until translucent, then stir in the chopped garlic and sage. As soon as the garlic becomes aromatic, add the wine and the lemon juice. Raise the heat to high and cook, stirring constantly and scraping the base of the pan to incorporate any sediment into the pan juices.

**4** Pour the pan juices over the meat and add the stock. Sprinkle over salt and pepper to taste, then add the finely chopped parsley.

**5** Bring to the boil, lower the heat, cover and simmer for 45–50 minutes, until the meat is tender and the sauce is a velvety consistency. Serve at once.

**Beating out veal**
Escalopes are thin slices of veal, cut from the leg. If they are a bit thick, it may be necessary to place them between sheets of clear film (plastic wrap) and beat them with a meat mallet. Thin slices of pork can be cooked in the same way.

1 shoulder of lamb, most of the fat
    removed, sliced into serving portions
600g/1lb 6oz ripe tomatoes, peeled and
    chopped or 400g/14oz can chopped
    plum tomatoes
4–5 garlic cloves, chopped
75ml/5 tbsp extra virgin olive oil
5ml/1 tsp dried oregano
1 litre/1¾ pints/4 cups hot water
400g/14oz/3½ cups orzo pasta, or
    spaghetti, broken into short lengths
salt and ground black pepper
50g/2oz/½ cup freshly grated Kefalotyri
    or Parmesan cheese, to serve

**Serves 6**

# baked lamb with tomatoes, garlic and pasta

arnaki yiouvetsi

A lamb yiouvetsi is undoubtedly very special in Greece. It is one of the most popular dishes and is often made for the celebratory family lunch on 15 August, after the long fasting period.

This date is important in the Greek Orthodox calendar as it marks the Feast of the Assumption of the Virgin Mary. It is particularly poignant for people who are called Maria, Despoina, Panagiota or Panagiotis – all popular names with Greeks – since they celebrate their name day (the equivalent of birthdays) on this occasion. As every family is bound to have at least one member named after the Virgin Mary, this calls for great celebration.

1 Preheat the oven to 190°C/375°F/Gas 5. Rinse the meat to remove any obvious bone splinters and place it in a large roasting pan.

2 Add the fresh or canned tomatoes, with the garlic, olive oil and oregano. Season with salt and pepper and stir in 300ml/½ pint/1¼ cups of the hot water.

3 Place the lamb in the oven and bake for about 1 hour 10 minutes, basting and turning the pieces of meat over a couple of times.

4 Reduce the oven temperature to 180°C/350°F/Gas 4. Add the remaining 700ml/scant 1¼ pints/2¾ cups hot water to the roasting pan. Stir in the pasta and add more seasoning. Mix well, return the roasting pan to the oven and bake for 30–40 minutes more, stirring occasionally, until the meat is fully cooked and tender and the pasta feels soft.

5 Serve immediately, with a bowl of grated cheese to be sprinkled over individual portions.

### Serve with a refreshing accompaniment

As yiouvetsi is quite a rich dish, it is imperative to accompany it with a salad, to refresh the palate.

### Try these ingredient variations

If possible, use ripe vine tomatoes, as it is their flavour that really makes the difference. The dish can also be made with young goat (kid) or beef, but these have to be boiled first.

1 small shoulder of lamb, boned and with
   most of the fat removed
2–3 onions, preferably red onions,
   quartered
2 red or green (bell) peppers, quartered
   and seeded
75ml/5 tbsp extra virgin olive oil
juice of 1 lemon
2 garlic cloves, crushed
5ml/1 tsp dried oregano
2.5ml/½ tsp dried thyme or some sprigs
   of fresh thyme, chopped
salt and ground black pepper

**Serves 4**

# grilled skewered lamb
arni souvlakia

This used to be street food par excellence when we were growing up in Athens. It was a real treat for us on balmy evenings to walk to the corner shop for souvlakia. We would stand outside to eat them, still immersed in the tantalizing aroma of the barbecuing lamb. Lamb still makes the best souvlakia, but in Greece this has now largely been replaced by pork, which is considerably cheaper. Unfortunately, the taste has suffered, as there is nothing to match the succulence and flavour of barbecued lamb.

Souvlakia are at their best served with tzatziki, a large tomato salad and barbecued bread.

**1** Ask your butcher to trim the meat and cut it into 4cm/1½in cubes. A little fat is desirable with souvlakia, as it keeps them moist and succulent during cooking. Separate the onion quarters into pieces, each composed of two or three layers, and slice each pepper quarter in half widthways.

**2** Put the oil, lemon juice, garlic and herbs in a large bowl. Season with salt and pepper and whisk well to combine. Add the meat cubes, stirring to coat them in the mixture.

**3** Cover the bowl tightly and leave to marinate for 4–8 hours in the refrigerator, stirring several times.

**4** Lift out the meat cubes, reserving the marinade, and thread them on long metal skewers, alternating each piece of meat with a piece of pepper and a piece of onion. Lay them across a grill pan or baking tray and brush them with the reserved marinade.

**5** Preheat a grill (broiler) until hot or prepare a barbecue. Cook the souvlakia under a medium to high heat or over the hot coals for 10 minutes, until they start to get scorched. If using the grill, do not place them too close to the heat source. Turn the skewers over, brush them again with the marinade (or a little olive oil) and cook them for 10–15 minutes more. They should be served immediately.

### Checking the cooking time
If you are barbecuing the souvlakia you may need to cook them for slightly longer, depending on the intensity of the heat.

### An alternative cut
If you prefer, you can use 4–5 best end neck fillets instead of shoulder.

60ml/4 tbsp extra virgin olive oil
1kg/2¼lb good-quality stewing steak or
   feather steak, sliced in 4 thick pieces
1 onion, chopped
2.5ml/½ tsp dried oregano
2 garlic cloves, chopped
1 glass white wine, about 175ml/6fl oz/
   ¾ cup
400g/14oz can chopped tomatoes
2–3 aubergines (eggplant), total weight
   about 675g/1½lb
150ml/¼ pint/⅔ cup sunflower oil
45ml/3 tbsp finely chopped fresh parsley
salt and ground black pepper

**Serves 4**

# beef and aubergine casserole
melitzanes me kreas

**Easy to make but with an exotic taste, this would make an excellent main course for a dinner party. Use good quality beef and cook it slowly, so that it is meltingly tender and full of flavour.**

**1** Heat the olive oil in a large pan and brown the pieces of meat on both sides. As each piece browns, take it out and set it aside on a plate.

**2** Add the chopped onion to the oil remaining in the pan and sauté it until translucent. Add the oregano and the garlic, then, as soon as the garlic becomes aromatic, return the meat to the pan and pour the wine over. Allow the wine to bubble and evaporate for a few minutes, then add the tomatoes, with enough hot water to just cover the meat. Bring to the boil, lower the heat, cover and cook for about 1 hour or a little longer, until the meat is tender.

**3** Meanwhile, trim the aubergines and slice them into 2cm/¾in thick rounds, then slice each round in half. Heat the sunflower oil and fry the aubergines briefly in batches over a high heat, turning them over as they become light golden. They do not have to cook at this stage and should not be allowed to burn. Lift them out and drain them on a platter lined with kitchen paper. When all the aubergines have been fried, season them.

**4** When the meat feels tender, season it, then add the aubergines and shake the pan to distribute them evenly. From this point, do not stir the mixture as the aubergines will be quite fragile. Add a little more hot water so that the aubergines are submerged in the sauce, cover the pan and simmer for 30 minutes more or until the meat is very tender and all the flavours have amalgamated. Sprinkle the parsley over the top and simmer for a few more minutes before serving with toasted pitta bread.

150g/5oz/⅔ cup unsalted (sweet) butter
115g/4oz/½ cup caster (superfine) sugar
4 eggs, separated
60ml/4 tbsp brandy
2.5ml/½ tsp ground cinnamon
300g/11oz/2¾ cups shelled walnuts
150g/5oz/1¼ cups self-raising
   (self-rising) flour
5ml/1 tsp baking powder
salt

**For the syrup**
250g/9oz/generous 1 cup caster
   (superfine) sugar
30ml/2 tbsp brandy
2–3 strips of pared orange rind
2 cinnamon sticks

**Serves 10–12**

# walnut cake
## karythopitta

This luscious cake is the finest Greek dessert of all. Its honey-soft texture, coupled with the sweetness of the walnuts, makes it irresistible.

On the islands it is traditionally made for name day celebrations, when any number of guests may drop in during the evening to convey their good wishes. Perfect for a large party, the cake tastes even better the day after it has been made.

**1** Preheat the oven to 190°C/375°F/Gas 5. Grease a 35 x 23cm/14 x 9in roasting pan or baking dish that is at least 5cm/2in deep. Cream the butter in a large mixing bowl until soft, then add the sugar and beat well until the mixture is light and fluffy.

**2** Add the egg yolks one by one, beating the mixture after each addition. Stir in the brandy and cinnamon. Coarsely chop the walnuts in a food processor and add them to the mixture. Mix in the walnuts using a wooden spoon. Do not use an electric mixer at this stage.

**3** Sift the flour with the baking powder and set aside. Whisk the egg whites with a pinch of salt until they are stiff. Fold them into the creamed mixture, alternating with tablespoons of flour until they and the flour have all been incorporated.

**4** Spread the mixture evenly in the prepared pan or dish. It should be about 4cm/1½in deep. Bake for about 40 minutes, until the top is golden and a skewer inserted in the cake comes out clean. Take the cake out of the oven and let it rest in the pan or dish while you make the syrup.

**5** Mix the sugar and 300ml/½ pint/1¼ cups water in a small pan. Heat gently, stirring, until the sugar has dissolved. Bring to the boil, lower the heat and add the brandy, orange rind and cinnamon sticks. Simmer for 10 minutes.

**6** Slice the karythopitta into 6cm/2½in diamond or square shapes while still hot and strain the syrup slowly over it. Let it stand for 10–20 minutes until it has absorbed the syrup and is thoroughly soaked.

### Keeping and serving
The cake will stay moist for 2–3 days, provided it is covered with clear film (plastic wrap), and does not need to go into the refrigerator unless the weather is very hot. It is traditional to offer a slice with a cup of coffee or a small glass of brandy.

# autumn

delectable pine nuts, golden quinces
and fresh, ripe green olives

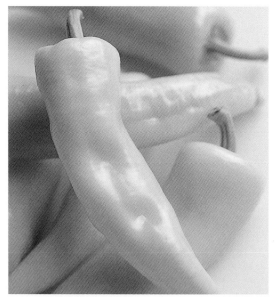

## As the end of August approaches

and as the sun begins to lose its dazzling brilliance, the first sign of the impending autumn is the sudden, eerie stillness in the olive groves (and even in our small garden) as the cicadas stop singing. After the season of excess comes the season of mellowness. The cooking deserts the garden and returns to the kitchen as the days get shorter and barbecues are packed away until the spring.

The excitement isn't over, however, for September is the month of the tuna run. More and more of the glistening silver fish are unloaded on island quays. Tuna seems to be at its best – and cheapest – at this time, and soon every household is enjoying baked tuna with potatoes, tomatoes and garlic.

The first green olives are harvested in early autumn, and are quickly cracked and cured, for Greeks love the refreshing taste of green olives. They are partial to pomegranates, too, and willingly brave the thorns on the tangled trees to pick the juicy, scarlet fruit.

September is the month for spetzofai – the Pelion speciality made up of mounds of elongated green peppers and garlic sausages. Peppers also feature in briami, a delicious bake that also includes courgettes (zucchini), potatoes, garlic and tomatoes.

At the end of September, the first supplies of gigantes – the giant dried beans that are widely used in winter dishes – arrive in the stores, a cause for rejoicing. The evenings are becoming chilly now, and the soup pan is again in evidence. Chicken soup is a favourite at this time of year, with lentil soup on Fridays. Life has definitely moved indoors, and the kitchen adapts itself to the change.

**Opposite**
Mellow-flavoured autumn ingredients, clockwise from top left: peppery rocket, elongated peppers, chicken in the pot ready to make avgolemono, fresh sausages, and gigantes (giant beans) baked with onions, tomatoes and parsley.

**Right**
A small motor cycle is laden with bundles of fresh flat leaf parsley ready for transport to the market in Chania on the island of Crete.

In late October, olive-picking starts in earnest, and the hillsides ring with the chatter and laughter of the pickers. Whole families come together under their olive trees, gathering the harvest that will produce the fresh and slightly peppery new season's oil. At about the same time, after the first rains, wild greenery is picked from the hillsides. Greeks love all kinds of horta (literally translated as "greens" ) and serve the wild leaves in all sorts of ways. They are particularly popular when lightly boiled and dressed with fruity green olive oil and lemon juice. Cultivated greens are sold in the shops and street markets, and are treated in precisely the same way. They form an important part of the autumn and winter diet in Greece.

There is a distinct chill in the air now, and the first stews start to be made. Combinations such as meat and cannellini beans, simmered slowly until meltingly tender, bring welcome warmth to the darker evenings.

**As the year begins to ebb**, there is one last blaze of golden colour to look forward to. The quince trees have shed their leaves, but hanging from their bare branches are huge, golden fruit. When I was a child, we used to eat quinces raw. My grandmother grated the fruit and sprinkled it with sugar and cinnamon, a treat that was almost on a par with eating pastokythono, quince paste, which wandering traders would sell in the streets of Athens every autumn. Quinces have a wonderful fragrance and flavour, and are delicious baked with lamb or beef in exotic casseroles for special Sunday lunches, or transformed into luscious, sweet spoon preserves to lift the spirits during the dark winter months.

Although Athens, like big cities everywhere, can cater to just about every culinary need, with a year-round supply of produce from all over the world, you have only to step outside the big food stores to find a world where local produce is still vitally important, and every season brings new delights for the cook. Here are some of autumn's treasures.

### Lemons

Like other citrus fruits, the lemon originated in South-east Asia and it reached Greece around the end of the 3rd century BC. Greeks love the flavour of lemons – a Greek kitchen without a bowl of lemons is an oddity – and of course, whenever possible, Greeks will plant a lemon tree in the garden. Lemon juice is squeezed generously into most dishes, but chief among its many uses, it is combined with olive oil as a dressing for salads, and blended with eggs to make the classic sauce, avgolemono.

### Quinces

With their rounded, silver leaves and large pink flowers, quince trees (cydonia oblonga) look beautiful in the spring, but in October, when only the golden fruits remain on the bare branches, they are truly entrancing. Quinces look a bit like elongated apples and can be as big as melons. They can be quite difficult to cut open. Inside there is a central core with brown seeds that is surrounded by golden flesh. When cooked, this turns a delicate shade of pink.

**Left**
Golden-skinned and with a wonderful fragrance and flavour, quinces are cooked in both savoury and sweet dishes.

**Above**
Lemons are loved by Greeks and the juice is used in all manner of dishes from salads to sauces.

### Avgolemono

This egg and lemon sauce is fundamental to Greek cooking, and gives an unforgettable flavour to dishes in which it is incorporated. Individual recipes give instructions for avgolemono, but here is a basic method for recipes to serve four.

• Beat 2 large (US extra large) eggs, at room temperature, in a bowl, then beat in the juice of 1–2 lemons and 5ml/1 tsp cornflour (cornstarch), mixed to a smooth cream with a little water.

• Add a ladleful of the hot soup (or stock or cooking sauce) and beat for 1 minute.

• Continue to beat the egg mixture while adding a second ladleful of hot liquid, then gradually add the contents of the bowl to the soup, stock or cooking sauce, stirring vigorously all the time.

• Warm the mixture over a gentle heat for no more than 1 or 2 minutes. Any longer and the eggs may curdle, even though the cornflour mixture will have helped to stabilize the sauce. Season to taste with salt before serving.

### Flat leaf parsley

Parsley originated in the eastern Mediterranean region and was widely used in ancient Greece and Rome, although it was mostly made into wreaths for athletes, rather than added to the cooking pot. Herbs such as oregano and thyme are more strongly identified with Greek cooking, but parsley is actually the most commonly used fresh herb. The flat leaf variety, which has a stronger scent and flavour than curly-leafed parsley, is used all year. Parsley is often coarsely chopped and added to shredded cabbage or tomato salads. It is essential for rustic bean and lentil soups, and is often combined with sage and spices to flavour chickpea rissoles. Parsley is an indispensable ingredient in vegetable dishes such as briami (courgette and potato bake) and dolmathes (stuffed vine leaves).

**Above**
Flat leaf parsley is the most commonly used herb in Greek cooking and is an essential flavouring ingredient in briami, a favourite oven-baked casserole made with sliced courgettes (zucchini) and potatoes.

### Rocket

Americans call it arugula, others know it as rocket, but in Greece it is called roka. The serrated green leaves have a strong, peppery taste and are very good to eat. Rocket grows like a weed, but quickly goes to seed and should be harvested young. Tender leaves are often served whole in Greece, perhaps with little red radishes or slices of feta cheese. More often, rocket is mixed with cos lettuce to make a tasty salad. Any coarse stems are trimmed and discarded, and the leaves are roughly chopped. Rocket is also added to other salads, especially potato salad, and gives an interesting edge to a mild-tasting dish.

### Pine nuts

These are the seeds that come from the cones of a pine tree, pinus pinea, indigenous to the Mediterranean region. They have a delicately sweet and deliciously creamy taste that adds flavour to all sorts of dishes.

**Above**
Rocket (arugula) is often mixed with cos lettuce for a salad.

**Right**
Purple-skinned Kalamata olives have a flavour that hints of red wine vinegar.

### Olives

If there is one tree which everyone immediately associates with Greece, it is the olive, olea europaea. Both olives and olive oil were staple foods in ancient Greece, and it was the ancient seafaring Greeks who introduced the olive tree to Italy, Spain and Provence.

Olives are inedible when first picked, as they taste incredibly bitter. Before they can be prepared for the table, they must be cracked or sliced and then immersed in cold water. The water must be changed daily for 10–15 days, after which time they will have lost their bitterness and will be ready for preserving in brine or oil, often with spices or aromatics.

Among the best-known Greek olives are those from Kalamata. Juicy and full of flavour, they have purple skins and a flavour that hints at the red wine vinegar used to cure them. Black olives, which are the fully ripe fruit, are grown all over Greece. The most common ones are small and wrinkly, and can taste slightly salty, but the large black Amphissa olives are very tasty. Green (unripe) olives are much loved by the Greeks, who value their fresh flavour.

### Olive oil

Greece is the third largest producer of extra olive oil, after Spain and Italy, and makes wonderful-tasting olive oil at competitive prices. Greeks consume more olive oil per capita than any other nation – 20kg (44lb) per annum.

Greek olive oil has both the colour – golden-green – and the taste of the fruit. Among the best Greek olive oils is the cold-pressed extra virgin oil called Mani, which is made from Koroneiki olives in the wild area in the south of the Peloponnese. There is also an organic version, which is superb and is a fraction of the cost of similar products. Look out, too, for Iliada, also from the Peloponnese. Olive oil from Crete is delicious, especially that which is marketed by the co-operative of Kolymbari.

### Feta cheese

Greek feta is a fresh, brilliant white cheese made from ewes' or goats' milk. The texture is interesting – soft, yet firm enough to cut in cubes – and it is stored in brine. It should have a lightly salty flavour, with a strong aftertaste, and can be extremely appetizing.

In Greece, feta is served on every conceivable occasion, from breakfast through to dinner, in both sweet and savoury contexts. Perhaps its most distinctive role is in horiatiki salad, when it is served with tomatoes, cucumber, onion and olives, but you will also find it served with slices of scarlet watermelon or with juicy figs. Small cubes of feta will often accompany a karafaki, a small glass of ouzo, the famous anise-flavoured Greek aperitif.

Feta is also crumbled and used with spinach or courgettes (zucchini) as a filling for the pies that are particularly popular in the autumn.

**Top right**
Golden-green olive oil is used in a huge range of Greek dishes, from roasts and vegetables to salad dressings and marinades.

**Middle right**
The perfect feta cheese: salty, crumbly and perfectly white.

**Bottom right**
Combined with almonds and semolina, sweet and creamy pine nuts make a delicious base for a cake.

1 large (US extra large) egg, plus 1 egg yolk
   for glazing
150g/5oz feta cheese
30ml/2 tbsp milk
30ml/2 tbsp chopped fresh mint leaves
15ml/1 tbsp raisins
15ml/1 tbsp pine nuts, lightly toasted
a little vegetable oil, for greasing

**For the pastry**
225g/8oz/2 cups self-raising
   (self-rising) flour
45ml/3 tbsp extra virgin olive oil
15g/½oz/1 tbsp butter, melted
90g/3½oz Greek (strained plain) yogurt

**Makes 12–14**

# half-moon cheese pies with raisins and pine nuts
skaltsounakia

These delicious small pies always dazzle
people. In Crete, where they are very popular,
there are several variations, including one
with a filling of sautéed wild greens.
Skaltsounakia can be offered with drinks or
presented as part of a large meze table.

**1** To make the pastry, put the flour in a bowl
and mix in the oil, butter and yogurt by hand.
Cover and rest in the refrigerator for 15 minutes.

**2** Meanwhile, make the filling. Beat the egg
lightly in a bowl. Crumble in the cheese, then
mix in the milk, mint, raisins and pine nuts.

**3** Preheat the oven to 190°C/375°F/Gas 5.
Cover half of the pastry, thinly roll out the
remainder and cut out 7.5cm/3in rounds.

**4** Place a heaped teaspoon of filling on each
round and fold the pastry over to make a half-
moon shape. Press the edges to seal, then place
the pies on a greased baking sheet. Repeat
with the remaining pastry. Brush the pies with egg
yolk and bake for 20 minutes, or until golden.

1 yellow or green elongated or
   bell-shaped pepper
1–2 fresh green chillies
200g/7oz feta cheese, cubed
60ml/4 tbsp extra virgin olive oil
juice of 1 lemon
45–60ml/3–4 tbsp milk
ground black pepper
a little finely chopped fresh flat
   leaf parsley, to garnish
slices of toast, to serve

**Serves 4**

# feta and roast pepper dip with chillies
htipiti

This is a familiar meze in the beautiful city of Thessalonika. If you stop for an ouzo in the area called Lathathika, that used to be part of the old market but now teems with trendy bars and restaurants, you will inevitably be served a small plate of htipiti. The dip is almost unknown elsewhere in Greece. This recipe comes from my brother-in-law, Kostas Printzios, who hails from Thessalonika.

**1** Scorch the pepper and chillies by threading them on metal skewers and turning them over a flame or under the grill (broiler), until charred all over.

**2** Set the pepper and chillies aside until cool enough to handle. Peel off as much of their skin as possible and wipe the blackened bits off with kitchen paper. Slit the pepper and chillies and discard the seeds and stem.

**3** Put the pepper and chilli flesh into a food processor. Add the other ingredients except the parsley and blend, adding a little more milk if too stiff. Spread on slices of toast, sprinkle a hint of parsley on top and serve.

300g/11oz/scant 1½ cups chickpeas,
    soaked overnight in water to cover
105ml/7 tbsp extra virgin olive oil
2 large onions, chopped
15ml/1 tbsp ground cumin
2 garlic cloves, crushed
3–4 fresh sage leaves, chopped
45ml/3 tbsp chopped flat leaf parsley
1 large (US extra large) egg, lightly beaten
45ml/3 tbsp self-raising (self-rising) flour
50g/2oz/½ cup plain (all-purpose) flour
radishes, rocket (arugula) and olives,
    to serve

**Serves 4**

# chickpea rissoles
revythokeftethes

This is one of the frugal mezethes that are typically found on a Greek table. Although the rissoles are very inexpensive to make, they are also very appetizing.

If you like, you can serve them with cauliflower with egg and lemon sauce or wilted spinach with rice and dill to make a complete and unusual vegetarian meal. The chickpea rissoles can also be served solo with drinks as mezethes or they can form part of a larger meze table. Radishes, rocket and olives are the traditional accompaniments.

**1** Drain the chickpeas, rinse them under cold water and drain again. Tip them into a large pan, cover with plenty of fresh cold water and bring them to the boil. Skim the froth from the surface of the water with a slotted spoon until the liquid is clear.

**2** Cover the pan and cook for 1¼–1½ hours, or until the chickpeas are very soft. Alternatively (and this is the better method) cook them in a pressure cooker under full pressure for 20–25 minutes. Once the chickpeas are soft, set aside a few tablespoons of the liquid from the chickpeas, then strain them, discarding the rest of the liquid. Tip the chickpeas into a food processor, add 30–45ml/2–3 tbsp of the reserved liquid and process to a velvety mash.

**3** Heat 45ml/3 tbsp of the olive oil in a large frying pan, add the onions and sauté until they are light golden. Add the cumin and the garlic and stir for a few seconds until their aroma rises. Stir in the chopped sage leaves and the parsley and set aside.

**4** Scrape the chickpea mash into a large bowl and add the egg, the self-raising flour and the fried onion and herb mixture. Add plenty of salt and pepper and mix well. Take large walnut-size pieces of the mixture and flatten them so that they look like thick, round mini-hamburgers.

**5** Coat the rissoles lightly in the plain flour. Heat the remaining olive oil in a large frying pan and fry them in batches until they are crisp and golden on both sides. Drain on kitchen paper and serve hot with the radishes, rocket and olives.

### Making shaping simple
Wet your hands slightly when shaping the mixture, as this helps to prevent the mixture from sticking to them.

1 chicken, about 1.6kg/3½lb
1.75 litres/3 pints/7½ cups water
2 onions, halved
2 carrots
3 celery sticks, each sliced into 3–4 pieces
a few flat leaf parsley sprigs
3–4 black peppercorns
50g/2oz/generous ⅓ cup short grain rice
salt

**For the egg and lemon sauce**
5ml/1 tsp cornflour (cornstarch)
2 large (US extra large) eggs, at room
   temperature
juice of 1–2 lemons

**Serves 4–6**

# chicken soup with egg and lemon sauce

kotopoulo soupa avgolemono

**Avgolemono has to be one of the most delicious and nourishing soups in the world. It fills me with nostalgia because it reminds me of autumnal lunches at home in Athens, where huge quantities were consumed. Its welcoming aroma always adds a bright note to a cold day, and it makes a very substantial meal by itself.**

1 Place the chicken in a large pan with the water. Bring to the boil and skim using a slotted spoon until the surface of the liquid is clear. Add the vegetables, parsley and peppercorns, season with salt and bring to the boil. Lower the heat slightly, then cover the pan and cook for 1 hour (longer if a boiling fowl or stewing chicken is used) until the chicken is very tender.

2 Carefully lift out the chicken and put it on a board or large plate. Strain the stock and set it aside, but discard the vegetables. Pull away the chicken breasts, skin them and dice the flesh. Do the same with the legs. Pour the stock back into the pan and add the chicken meat.

3 Shortly before serving, heat the stock and diced chicken. When the stock boils, add the rice.

4 Cover the pan and cook for about 8 minutes, until soft. Take the pan off the heat and let the soup cool a little before adding the sauce.

5 Make the sauce. Mix the cornflour to a paste with a little water. Beat the eggs in a bowl, add the lemon juice and the cornflour mixture and beat together until smooth and well mixed. Gradually beat a ladleful of the chicken stock into the egg mixture, then continue to beat for 1 minute. Add a second ladleful in the same way. By now the sauce will be warm so you can pour it slowly into the soup, and stir vigorously to mix it in.

6 Warm the soup over a gentle heat for no more than 1–2 minutes. Any longer and the eggs may curdle, even though the cornflour should safeguard against that happening. Serve immediately, with a plate of lemon quarters for those who wish to add extra juice.

### Choosing the right chicken

The soup will have much more character if either a boiling fowl or a large organic chicken is used. The chicken soup (without the rice) can be made well in advance; up to a day before it is needed. Cool it quickly and keep it in a covered bowl in the refrigerator.

275g/10oz/1¼ cups brown-green lentils,
    preferably the small variety
150ml/¼ pint/⅔ cup extra virgin olive oil
1 onion, thinly sliced
2 garlic cloves, sliced into
    thin batons
1 carrot, sliced into thin discs
400g/14oz can chopped tomatoes
15ml/1 tbsp tomato purée (paste)
2.5ml/½ tsp dried oregano
1 litre/1¾ pints/4 cups hot water
salt and ground black pepper
30ml/2 tbsp roughly chopped fresh herb
    leaves, to garnish

**Serves 4**

# lentil soup
## faki soupa

Lentils are a winter staple in Greece and very delicious they are too. As they do not need soaking, they make an easy option for a quick meal. The secret of good lentil soup, as with all these winter dishes from Greece, is to be generous with the olive oil. The soup is served as a main meal, accompanied by olives, bread and cheese or, for a special occasion, with fried squid or keftethes.

**1** Rinse the lentils, drain them and put them in a large pan with cold water to cover. Bring to the boil and boil for 3–4 minutes. Strain, discarding the liquid, and set the lentils aside.

**2** Wipe the pan clean, heat the olive oil in it, then add the onion and sauté until translucent. Stir in the garlic, then, as soon as it becomes aromatic, return the lentils to the pan. Add the carrot, tomatoes, tomato purée and oregano. Stir in the hot water and a little pepper to taste.

**3** Bring to the boil, then lower the heat, cover the pan and cook gently for 20–30 minutes until the lentils feel soft but have not begun to disintegrate. Add salt and the chopped herbs just before serving.

500g/1¼lb minced (ground) beef or lamb
1 onion, grated
1 egg, lightly beaten
50g/2oz/generous ⅓ cup short
   grain rice
45ml/3 tbsp chopped flat leaf parsley
finely grated rind of ½ orange, plus extra
   to garnish (optional)
salt and ground black pepper

**For the sauce**
60ml/4 tbsp extra virgin olive oil
1 onion, thinly sliced
3–4 fresh sage leaves, finely sliced
400g/14oz can tomatoes
300ml/½ pint/1¼ cups beef stock
   or hot water

**Serves 4**

# meatballs in rich tomato sauce
## yiouvarlakia

**This is a practical all-in-one dish that is very easy to make. There are different versions of it, but in the autumn I prefer the tomato sauce as it seems to bring back shades of summer with its sweetness.**

**1** Put the meat in a bowl and add the onion, egg, rice and parsley. Add the grated orange rind to the mixture with salt and pepper. Mix all the ingredients well, then shape the mixture into round balls or small sausage shapes.

**2** Make the sauce. Heat the oil in a wide pan that will take the meatballs in one layer. Sauté the onion slices until they just start to become golden. Add the sage, then the tomatoes, breaking them up with a wooden spoon.

**3** Simmer for a few minutes, then add the stock or water and bring to the boil. Lower the yiouvarlakia gently into the sauce. Do not stir but rotate the pan to coat evenly. Season, then cover the pan and simmer for about 30 minutes until the sauce has thickened. Scatter over a little orange rind to garnish, if you like. Serve with lots of crusty bread to mop up the juices.

225g/8oz/1 cup Greek fava or yellow
  split peas
1.5 litres/2½ pints/6¼ cups water
1 onion, finely chopped
4 medium squid, total weight about
  900g/2lb
50g/2oz/½ cup plain (all-purpose) flour
75ml/5 tbsp olive oil or sunflower oil
2–3 shallots, finely chopped
60–75ml/4–5 tbsp extra virgin olive oil
juice of ½ lemon
salt and ground black pepper
15ml/1 tbsp finely chopped fresh parsley,
  to garnish

**Serves 4**

# split pea purée with fried squid
fava me kalamarakia

For a long time, this frugal dish was abandoned by Greeks, as it reminded them of the Second World War and the difficult years that followed. However, the last 10 years have seen a resurgence in its popularity, and fava is now to be found on most restaurant menus in Greece. It is traditionally served very simply scattered with chopped onion and parsley and drizzled with olive oil, but in this recipe I have served it with fried squid.

**1** Soak the fava or split peas in cold water to cover for 1 hour. Tip into a sieve, rinse several times, then drain and place in a large heavy pan. Pour in the measured water. Bring to the boil and skim, using a slotted spoon, until the liquid is clear.

**2** Add the chopped onion and simmer uncovered for 1 hour or more, depending on the age of the peas, stirring occasionally. Towards the end of the cooking time, watch the mixture closely as it may start to stick. Once cooked, the peas should be perfectly soft and moist. Stir in salt to taste.

**3** Meanwhile, prepare the squid, following the instructions in the introduction to the winter chapter, but keep the bodies intact. Rinse them thoroughly, inside and out, and drain well.

**4** Season the flour with salt and pepper then toss the squid in it until evenly coated.

**5** Purée the pea mixture in a food processor while it is still hot as it will solidify when cold. The purée should be smooth and have the consistency of thick cream.

**6** Heat the olive or sunflower oil in a large frying pan. When it is hot enough to sizzle but is not smoking, add the squid bodies, without letting them touch each other. Cook until pale golden underneath, then turn and cook until they are pale golden all over. Add the tentacles and cook until they are golden all over.

**7** Spread the pea mixture on individual plates in a thin layer and let it cool a little. Sprinkle the chopped shallots evenly over the top, then drizzle with the virgin olive oil and lemon juice. Add the fried squid. Grind a little pepper over and add the chopped parsley and lemon wedges. Fava can be served warm or at room temperature.

### Try to buy the real thing
If you can find them, do try to use the Greek pulses known, like the dish itself, as fava. They are smaller than ordinary yellow split peas and have a sweeter taste. Pick them over before cooking and remove any small stones and grit.

400g/14oz/1¼ cups Greek fasolia gigantes
   or similar large dried white beans
150ml/¼ pint/⅔ cup extra virgin olive oil
2–3 onions, total weight about
   300g/11oz, chopped
1 celery stick, thinly sliced
2 carrots, cubed
3 garlic cloves, thinly sliced
5ml/1 tsp each dried oregano and thyme
400g/14oz can chopped tomatoes
30ml/2 tbsp tomato purée (paste) diluted
   in 300ml/½ pint/1¼ cups hot water
2.5ml/½ tsp granulated sugar
45ml/3 tbsp finely chopped flat
   leaf parsley
salt and ground black pepper

**Serves 4 as a main course**
**6 as a first course**

# giant beans baked with tomatoes
## gigantes fournou

Gigantes are a type of white bean, resembling butter beans, but larger, rounder and much sweeter. They come from the north of Greece and the best come from Kastoria. Similar beans are found in Italy and Spain. In major cities outside Greece, look for them in specialist food stores. They make a delicious dish, which is often to be found in tavernas in Greece, even in the summer. Gigantes fournou usually forms part of the meze in a Greek restaurant but is more likely to be served as a main course for a family meal.

1 Place the beans in a large bowl, cover with plenty of cold water, then leave the beans to soak overnight. The next day, drain the beans, then rinse them under cold water and drain again. Tip the beans into a large pan, pour in plenty of water to cover, then bring to the boil. Cover the pan and cook the beans until they are almost tender. Gigantes are not like other beans – they cook quickly, so keep testing the beans after they have cooked for 30–40 minutes. They should not be allowed to disintegrate from overcooking.

2 When the beans are cooked, tip them into a colander to drain, discarding the cooking liquid, then set them aside. Preheat the oven to 180°C/350°F/Gas 4.

3 Heat the olive oil in the clean pan, add the onions and sauté until light golden. Add the celery, carrots, garlic and dried herbs and stir with a wooden spatula until the garlic becomes aromatic.

4 Stir in the tomatoes, cover and cook for 10 minutes. Pour in the diluted tomato purée, then return the beans to the pan. Stir in the sugar and parsley, with plenty of salt and pepper.

5 Tip the bean mixture into a baking dish and bake for 30 minutes, checking the beans once or twice and adding more hot water if they look dry. The surface should be slightly scorched and sugary.

**Avoid adding salt**
Never add salt to dried beans or pulses of any kind before they are cooked, as it makes their skin leathery.

675g/1½lb courgettes (zucchini)
450g/1lb potatoes, peeled and cut
    into chunks
1 onion, finely sliced
3 garlic cloves, chopped
1 large red (bell) pepper, seeded
    and cubed
400g/14oz can chopped tomatoes
150ml/¼ pint/⅔ cup extra virgin olive oil
150ml/¼ pint/⅔ cup hot water
5ml/1 tsp dried oregano
45ml/3 tbsp chopped fresh flat
    leaf parsley
salt and ground black pepper

**Serves 4 as a main course**
**6 as a first course**

# courgette and potato bake
briami

Cook this delicious dish in early autumn,
and the aromas spilling from the kitchen will
recall the rich summer tastes and colours
just passed. Briami is very easy to make and
everyone loves it, including children. It is
especially mouthwatering when the potatoes
on top are lightly scorched. In Greece, this
would constitute a main meal, with a salad,
some olives and cheese. It can be served
hot or at room temperature.

**1** Preheat the oven to 190°C/375°F/Gas 5.
Scrape the courgettes lightly under running
water to dislodge any grit and then slice them
into thin rounds. Put them in a large baking
dish and add the potatoes, onion, garlic, red
pepper and tomatoes. Mix well, then stir in the
oil, hot water and oregano.

**2** Spread the mixture evenly, then season with
salt and pepper. Bake for 30 minutes, then stir
in the parsley and a little more water.

**3** Return the bake to the oven and cook for
1 hour more, increasing the oven temperature to
200°C/400°F/Gas 6 for the final 10–15 minutes,
so that the potatoes brown.

a large handful of rocket (arugula) leaves
2 cos (romaine) lettuce hearts
3–4 fresh flat leaf parsley sprigs,
    coarsely chopped
30–45ml/2–3 tbsp finely chopped
    fresh dill
75ml/5 tbsp extra virgin olive oil
15–30ml/1–2 tbsp lemon juice
salt

**Serves 4**

# wild rocket and cos lettuce salad

maroulosalata me roka

Salads in Greece are clean-tasting and often quite lemony in flavour. The national preference for strong-tasting leaves – sometimes quite bitter ones – is also reflected in fresh salads. Wild rocket is a favourite ingredient, added to give salads a sharp new edge.

**1** If the rocket leaves are young and tender they can be left whole but older ones should be trimmed of thick stalks and then sliced coarsely.

**2** Slice the cos lettuce in thin ribbons and place these in a bowl, then add the rocket and the chopped parsley and dill.

**3** Make a dressing by whisking the oil and lemon juice with salt to taste in a bowl until the mixture emulsifies and thickens. Just before serving, pour over the dressing and toss lightly to coat everything in the glistening oil.

**Achieving the perfect balance**
It is important to balance the bitterness of the rocket and the sweetness of the cos lettuce, and the best way to find out if the balance is right is by taste.

105ml/7 tbsp extra virgin olive oil
juice of 1 large lemon
3 garlic cloves, crushed
4 medium-thick tuna steaks, total
   weight about 800g/1¾lb
45ml/3 tbsp chopped fresh flat
   leaf parsley
15ml/1 tbsp fresh oregano or
   5ml/1 tsp dried
500g/1¼lb potatoes, peeled and cut
   into small cubes
450g/1lb ripe tomatoes, peeled
   and chopped
150ml/¼ pint/⅔ cup hot water
salt and ground black pepper

**Serves 4**

# baked tuna with golden brown potatoes
## tonos plaki

September is the month when the fishermen on Alonnisos land their biggest catches of tuna, and is also the time when the local women are hard at work making this dish. It is traditional to the island and is often cooked in the ovens of the local baker, after the final batch of bread has been made. At lunchtime, the aromas of garlic and oregano are simply intoxicating.

**1** Mix the olive oil with the lemon juice and garlic, in a shallow dish that will hold all the tuna steaks in a single layer. Stir in salt and pepper, then add the tuna steaks. Scatter over the herbs and turn the steaks to coat them in the marinade. Leave to marinate for 1–2 hours. Lift the steaks out and lay them in a roasting pan.

**2** Preheat the oven to 180°C/350°F/Gas 4. Drop the cubes of potato into the marinating dish and turn them to coat them in the olive oil mixture. Arrange them around the tuna steaks, drizzle over any remaining marinade and sprinkle the chopped tomatoes on top.

**3** Pour the hot water into the roasting pan. Bake the tuna for 40 minutes, turning it over halfway through and stirring the potatoes.

**4** Transfer the tuna to a heated platter and cover it with foil to keep it warm. Increase the oven temperature to 200°C/400°F/Gas 6, add a little more hot water to the roasting pan if needed and cook the potatoes for about 15 minutes more to brown them and make them crisp. Serve the tuna and potato mixture with an imaginative green salad, if you like.

500g/1¼lb fresh spinach, trimmed of
   thick stalks
4 x 200g/7oz fresh hake steaks or 4 pieces
   of cod fillet
30ml/2 tbsp plain (all-purpose) flour
75ml/5 tbsp extra virgin olive oil
1 glass white wine (175ml/6fl oz/¾ cup)
3–4 strips of pared lemon rind
salt and ground black pepper

**For the egg and lemon sauce**
2 large (US extra large) eggs at room
   temperature
juice of ½ lemon
2.5ml/½ tsp cornflour (cornstarch)

**Serves 4**

# hake with spinach and egg and lemon sauce
bakaliaros me spanaki avgolemono

Fish cooked with various greens has its roots in monastic life. Religious observance required that fish be eaten on certain days, such as the Annunciation of the Virgin on 25 March or Palm Sunday, and monastery cooks added interest to what might otherwise have been a bland meal. They included wild greens gathered from the hillsides – different ones according to the season.

In the modern kitchen, the wild greens have been substituted with vegetables such as spinach, celery, leeks, turnip tops and fennel. This simple, quick, delicious and healthy dish is a particular favourite of the Aegean islands.

1 Place the spinach leaves in a large pan with just the water that clings to the leaves after washing. Cover the pan tightly and cook over a medium heat for 5–7 minutes, until they are cooked. Remove the lid occasionally and turn the leaves using a wooden spoon. Drain and set the spinach aside.

2 Dust the fish lightly with the flour and shake off any excess. Heat the olive oil in a large frying pan, add the pieces of fish and sauté gently, for 2–3 minutes on each side, until the flesh starts to turn golden.

3 Pour the wine over the fish, add the lemon rind and some seasoning and carefully shake the pan from side to side to blend the flavourings. Lower the heat and simmer gently for a few minutes until the wine has reduced a little.

4 Add the spinach, distributing it evenly around the fish. Let it simmer for 3–4 minutes more, then pull the pan off the heat and let it stand for a few minutes before adding the sauce.

5 Prepare the egg and lemon sauce as described in the recipe for chicken soup with egg and lemon sauce, using the quantities listed here. Pour the sauce over the fish and spinach, place the pan over a very gentle heat and shake to amalgamate the ingredients. If it appears too dry add a little warm water. Allow to cook gently for 2–3 minutes and serve.

### Cleaning the spinach
Spinach can be gritty, especially if you pick it from your own garden. The best way to wash it is to swirl the leaves gently in a sink full of cold water, then lift them out by hand into a colander. Repeat the process four or five times until the water is clear.

675g/1½lb sweet peppers
75ml/5 tbsp extra virgin olive oil
500g/1¼lb spicy sausages (Italian garlic
    sausages, Merguez or Toulouse)
400g/14oz tomatoes, roughly sliced
5ml/1 tsp dried oregano or some fresh
    thyme, chopped
150ml/¼ pint/⅔ cup hot water
45ml/3 tbsp chopped flat leaf parsley
salt and ground black pepper

**Serves 4**

# spicy sausage and pepper stew
## spetzofai pilioritiko

This dish is a speciality of the Pelion, the beautiful mountain range that towers over the city of Volos on one side and the blue Aegean on the other, on the eastern coast of Greece. You will find spetzofai in all its picture-postcard villages. Visit Milies, Tsangaratha, Zagora or Makrinitsa and you will inevitably find it bubbling in the kitchen, but it is also popular on all the nearby islands of Skiathos, Alonnisos and Skopelos.

The peppers used traditionally in this recipe are the local thin, elongated yellow and green ones that are sweet. However, you can also use elongated red peppers or a mixture of the bell-shaped red, green and yellow peppers that are more commonly found.

**1** Halve and seed the peppers and cut them into quarters. Heat the olive oil in a large heavy pan, add the peppers and sauté them over a medium heat for 10–15 minutes until they start to brown.

**2** Meanwhile, slice the sausages into bitesize chunks. Carefully tip the hot olive oil into a frying pan. Add the sausages and fry them briefly, turning them frequently, to get rid of the excess fat but not to cook them. As soon as they are brown, remove the sausages from the pan with a slotted spoon and drain them on a plate lined with kitchen paper.

**3** Add the tomatoes, sausages and herbs to the peppers. Stir in the water and season with salt and pepper, then cover the pan and cook gently for about 30 minutes. Mix in the parsley and serve.

### An alternative cooking method

If you prefer, you can stir in the parsley, spread the mixture in a medium baking dish and bake it in an oven preheated to 180°C/350°F/Gas 4. Cook for about 40 minutes, stirring occasionally and adding more hot water when needed.

75ml/5 tbsp extra virgin olive oil
1 organic or free-range chicken, about
  1.6kg/3½lb, jointed
3–4 shallots, finely chopped
2 carrots, sliced
1 celery stick, roughly chopped
2 garlic cloves, chopped
juice of 1 lemon
300ml/½ pint/1¼ cups hot water
30ml/2 tbsp chopped flat
  leaf parsley
12 green or black olives
salt and ground black pepper

**Serves 4**

# chicken casserole with olives
kotopoulo me elies

**This is a very simple dish to prepare and cook but with its typical Mediterranean undertones it is also full of flavour. In our family, it was often served with French fries or plain boiled rice, but it goes equally well with boiled new potatoes.**

**1** Preheat the oven to 180°C/350°F/Gas 4. Heat the olive oil in a wide flameproof casserole and brown the chicken pieces on both sides. Lift them out and set them aside.

**2** Add the shallots, carrots and celery to the oil remaining in the casserole and sauté them for a few minutes until the shallots are glistening. Stir in the garlic. As soon as it becomes aromatic, return the chicken to the pan and pour the lemon juice over the mixture. Let it bubble for a few minutes, then add the water and season with salt and pepper.

**3** Cover the casserole and put it in the oven. Bake for 1 hour, turning the chicken pieces over occasionally. Remove the casserole from the oven, stir in the parsley and olives, mix well together, then recover the casserole and return it to the oven for about 30 minutes more.

4 lamb shanks
45ml/3 tbsp plain (all-purpose) flour
45ml/3 tbsp extra virgin olive oil
1 large onion, chopped
2 garlic cloves, sliced
1 celery stick, sliced
1 carrot, sliced
leaves from 2 fresh rosemary sprigs
2 bay leaves
175ml/6fl oz/¾ cup white wine
30ml/2 tbsp tomato purée (paste)
225g/8oz/1 cup dried cannellini beans,
   soaked overnight in water to cover
150ml/¼ pint/⅔ cup hot water
salt and ground black pepper

**Serves 4**

# lamb shanks with cannellini beans
## arnaki me fasolia

**Earthy and substantial, this is the ideal dish for chilly autumn evenings. The beans acquire layers of taste when slow-cooked in the rich sauce provided by the meat. All it needs to serve with it is a clean-tasting, lemon-dressed salad.**

**1** Preheat the oven to 160°C/325°F/Gas 3. Season the lamb shanks and coat them lightly in flour. Heat the oil in a large flameproof casserole over a high heat and brown the pieces of meat on all sides. Lift them out and set them aside.

**2** Add the onion to the oil remaining in the casserole and sauté gently. As soon as it is light golden, stir in the garlic, celery, carrot, rosemary and bay leaves.

**3** Put the meat back in the pan and pour the wine slowly over it. Let it bubble and reduce, then stir in the tomato purée diluted in about 450ml/¾ pint/scant 2 cups hot water. Drain the soaked beans and add them to the pan with black pepper to taste. Mix well. Cover the casserole, transfer it to the oven and bake for 1 hour. Stir in salt to taste and add the hot water. Cover and cook for 1 hour more, or until tender.

juice of ½ lemon
2–3 large quinces, total weight about
    1kg/2¼lb
75ml/5 tbsp extra virgin olive oil
1kg/2¼lb good quality feather beef steak
    (see tip below), cut in large slices
1 glass white wine, about 175ml/
    6fl oz/¾ cup
300ml/½ pint/1¼ cups hot water
1 cinnamon stick
45ml/3 tbsp demerara (raw) sugar mixed
    with 300ml/½ pint/1¼ cups hot water
1 whole nutmeg
salt

**Serves 4**

# beef with quinces
## moshari me kythonia

This is a very exotic dish, which always reminds me of mellow autumn days when the dazzling fruit hung from almost bare branches. In late October and early November the orchard looked as if it was filled with surreal Christmas trees. I love quinces for their aroma and complex flavours and I can eat them in all sorts of ways, but I also know that they are an acquired taste. However, in this combination of sweet and savoury flavours they win everyone over, including the uninitiated. You do not need to serve anything else with this dish.

1 Have ready a bowl of water acidulated with the lemon juice. Using a sharp cook's knife, quarter each quince vertically. Core and peel the pieces and drop them into the acidulated water to prevent them from discolouring.

2 Heat the olive oil in a large heavy pan. When it is almost smoking, brown the meat on both sides, turning the pieces over once. As soon as all the meat has browned, lower the heat, pour the wine over and let it bubble and reduce slightly.

3 Pour the hot water into the pan and add the cinnamon stick. Cover the pan and cook over a gentle heat for about 1 hour or until the meat is tender. Add salt to taste.

4 Lift the quinces out of the acidulated water, and slice each piece vertically into 2–3 elongated pieces. Spread half the quince slices in a single layer in a large frying pan, pour half the sugared water over and cook them gently for 10 minutes, turning them over occasionally until all the liquid has been absorbed and they start to brown and caramelize.

5 Spread the caramelized quince slices over the meat in the pan and repeat the caramelizing process with the remaining quince slices. Having added them to the meat, finely grate about one-quarter of a whole nutmeg over the top. If necessary, add more hot water to cover the quince slices.

6 Cover the pan and cook for 30 minutes more until both the meat and the quince slices are meltingly soft and sweet. Do not stir the mixture after the quince has been added; instead, shake the pan from side to side occasionally so that the meat is prevented from sticking to the base. Serve hot.

**Meat cuts**
Feather steak is a tender cut of beef, from between the neck and rib, near the chuck. It is particularly good for braising. If you can't find it, use stewing or braising steak instead.

2–3 medium slices of bread,
   crusts removed
675g/1½lb minced (ground) lamb or beef
2 garlic cloves, crushed
15ml/1 tbsp ground cumin
1 egg, lightly beaten
25g/1oz/¼ cup plain (all-purpose) flour
45ml/3 tbsp sunflower oil, for frying
salt and ground black pepper

**For the sauce**
45ml/3 tbsp olive oil
5ml/1 tsp cumin seeds
400g/14oz can chopped tomatoes
15ml/1 tbsp tomato purée (paste) diluted
   in 150ml/¼ pint/⅔ cup hot water
2.5ml/½ tsp dried oregano
12–16 green olives, preferably cracked
   ones, rinsed and drained

**Serves 4**

# meat rissoles with cumin and cracked green olives
soutzoukakia me elies

**A delicious dish that probably originated with the Greeks who came from Asia Minor after the catastrophic war with Turkey in 1922. It is ideal for entertaining as it can be cooked in advance and re-heated as needed. Serve the rissoles with plain rice, French fries or pasta.**

**1** Soak the bread in water for 10 minutes, then drain, squeeze dry and place in a large bowl. Add the meat, garlic, cumin and egg. Season with salt and pepper, then mix either with a fork or your hands, until blended.

**2** Take a small handful – the size of a large walnut – and roll it into a short, slim sausage. Set this aside. Continue until all the meat mixture has been used. Roll all the sausage-shaped rissoles lightly in flour, shaking each one to get rid of any excess.

**3** Heat the sunflower oil in a large non-stick frying pan and fry the soutzoukakia, in batches if necessary, until they are golden on all sides. Lift them out and place them in a bowl. Discard the oil remaining in the pan.

**4** Make the sauce. Heat the olive oil in a large pan. Add the cumin seeds and swirl them around for a few seconds until they are aromatic. Add the tomatoes and stir with a wooden spatula for about 2 minutes to break them up. Pour in the diluted tomato purée, mix well, then add the soutzoukakia. Stir in the oregano and olives, with salt and pepper to taste. Spoon the sauce over the soutzoukakia, then cover and cook gently for 30 minutes, shaking the pan occasionally to prevent them from sticking. Tip into a serving dish and serve.

**A seductive serving suggestion**
The soutzoukakia taste delicious when simmered in the cumin-flavoured tomato sauce, but their aroma is so seductive when they are first fried that you may not be able to wait that long. There's no reason why you shouldn't serve them on their own – just make certain that they are cooked through.

500g/1¼lb/2½ cups caster
   (superfine) sugar
1 litre/1¾ pints/4 cups cold water
1 cinnamon stick
250ml/8fl oz/1 cup olive oil
350g/12oz/2 cups coarse semolina
50g/2oz/½ cup blanched almonds
30ml/2 tbsp pine nuts
5ml/1 tsp ground cinnamon

**Serves 6–8**

# semolina cake
## halvas

Halvas is the universal family treat, loved by everyone in Greece. It takes very little time to make – about 20 minutes – and uses quite inexpensive ingredients that every Greek household routinely has. It makes a perfect accompaniment to Greek coffee. The popularity of halvas is reflected in its simple formula, which any Greek woman can recite: one, two, three, four. This refers to the number of cups of the essential ingredients: one of olive oil, two of semolina, three of sugar and four of water. This recipe has slightly less sugar, to appeal to contemporary tastes.

**1** Put the sugar in a heavy pan, pour in the water and add the cinnamon stick. Bring to the boil, stirring until the sugar dissolves, then boil without stirring for about 4 minutes to make a syrup.

**2** Meanwhile, heat the oil in a separate, heavy pan. When it is almost smoking, add the semolina gradually and stir continuously until it turns light brown.

**3** Lower the heat, add the almonds and pine nuts and brown together for 2–3 minutes, stirring continuously. Take the semolina mixture off the heat and set aside. Remove the cinnamon stick from the hot syrup using a slotted spoon and discard it.

**4** Protecting your hand with an oven glove or dishtowel, carefully add the hot syrup to the semolina mixture, stirring all the time. The mixture will hiss and spit at this point, so stand well away from it.

**5** Return the pan to a gentle heat and stir until all the syrup has been absorbed and the mixture looks smooth. Remove the pan from the heat, cover it with a clean dishtowel and let it stand for 10 minutes so that any remaining moisture is absorbed.

**6** Scrape the mixture into a 20–23cm/8–9in round cake tin (pan), preferably fluted, and set it aside. When it is cold, unmould it on to a platter and dust it all over with the ground cinnamon.

### Choosing the right oil
In Greece, this recipe would be made with extra virgin olive oil, but you may prefer the less dominant flavour of a light olive oil.

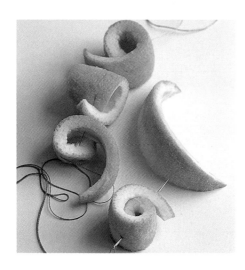 

8–9 thick-skinned oranges, total weight
about 1kg/2¼lb, rinsed and dried
1kg/2¼lb/4½ cups caster (superfine) sugar
juice of 1 lemon

**Makes about 30 pieces**

# orange spoon preserve
nerantzi glyko

Spoon preserves are made with various types of fruit in a luscious syrup. Figs, cherries, grapes and apricots are all suitable, as are small bitter oranges, which are left whole. You may also find preserved fresh green walnuts stuffed with whole cloves and almonds. A beautiful preserve is made from rose petals and some more unusual preserves are made from small aubergines or plum tomatoes.

I make orange peel preserve in late autumn with navel oranges and in winter I use Seville oranges. It is my favourite preserve as it is the easiest type to make and will happily keep for one or two years.

1 Grate the oranges lightly and discard the zest. Slice each one vertically into 4–6 pieces (depending on the size of the oranges), remove the peel from each segment, keeping it in one piece, and drop it into a bowl of cold water. Use the flesh in another recipe.

2 Have ready a tapestry needle threaded with strong cotton string. Roll up a piece of peel and push the needle through it so that it is threaded on the string. Continue this process until there are 10–12 pieces on the string, then tie the two ends together. String the remaining peel in the same way. Put the strings in a bowl of fresh cold water and leave for 24 hours, changing the water 3–4 times.

3 Next day, drain the strings of peel and put them in a large pan. Pour in about 2.8 litres/4½ pints/11 cups water. Bring to the boil, partially cover the pan and continue to boil for 15 minutes. Drain well. Return the strings of peel to the pan, cover with the same amount of water and boil for 10 minutes until the peel feels soft but not overcooked. Tip into a colander and leave to drain for at least 1 hour.

4 Put the sugar in a large heavy pan and add 150ml/ ¼ pint/⅔ cup water. Stir over a gentle heat until the sugar dissolves, then boil gently without stirring for about 4 minutes until it forms a thick syrup.  Release the fruit into the syrup by cutting the threads. Simmer for 5 minutes, then remove the pan from the heat and leave the peel to stand in the syrup overnight.

5 Next day, boil the syrup very gently for 4–5 minutes, until it starts to set. Stir in the lemon juice, take the pan off the heat and let the preserve cool. Pack the peel and syrup into sterilized jars. Seal and label, then store in a cool, dry place.

**How to serve**

This type of spoon preserve – glyko tou koutaliou – is often served to visitors. Offer one piece on a spoon, resting in a saucer, along with a glass of cold water.

# winter

ruby red beetroots, delicious dried
beans and comforting casseroles

**Throughout the winter**, the streets in Greek towns and villages are very often deserted and quiet, although the markets still operate on their prescribed days of the week. The summer visitors would no longer recognize the Greek islands, which now seem eerie and almost abandoned. Greek life has definitely moved indoors.

In the summer, it was the kitchens that were kept cool, while the weather outside was often incredibly hot. Now the reverse applies. As the temperature drops, kitchens become havens of comfort. This is the season when saucepans simmer quietly on stoves for much of the day, slowly transforming tough pulses into tender, tasty dishes. Dried beans, split peas, lentils and chickpeas are all used in this way, creating the casseroles that provide nourishment for the body and warmth to the house.

Cretan cooks aren't content to use just one type of pulse, but combine as many as they can find with whole grains of wheat to produce a simple, but magnificent, casserole with the wonderful name of pallikaria. The name means "brave ones", but whether that applies to the cooks or those who eat the dish is not clear.

The rest of Greece will almost certainly be devoting themselves to making the national (and extremely robust) bean soup called fasolatha, which has nourished and sustained Greeks for centuries. Essentially a frugal dish, fasolatha is traditionally accompanied by a plate of olives, quartered raw onions or garlic. For a special meal, it can be transformed with keftethes (fried meatballs) redolent of the aromas of the hillsides. Alternatively, fasolatha can be a prelude to the preserved fish that the Greeks love: lakertha (pickled white tuna) or salted anchovies. These are taken from huge tins, with the glistening salt flakes still clinging to them. After being rinsed, filleted and (if a milder flavour is preferred) marinated in milk for a short time, they are dressed with olive oil and a little lemon juice.

**Top left**
Beetroot is very popular in Greece and is often served with skorthalia, a strong-flavoured garlic sauce.

**Top right**
The Greeks love preserved fish and salted anchovies are a particular favourite, especially when dressed with olive oil.

**Left**
Cannellini beans, although not indigenous to Greece, have been popular for generations. They are the basis of the hearty soup, fasolatha, which is perhaps the most Greek of Greek dishes.

**Right**
Fasolatha, the national soup of Greece, is always served with a plate of olives, and wedges of raw onions or garlic.

**Below right**
The winter vegetable markets are much less colourful than those in summer, but there are still a few spots of colour – ruby beetroots and purple cabbages – to brighten the stalls.

In winter, the street markets are no longer multi-coloured but have become almost monochromatic. Green and white are the colours of the season. Slim leeks, creamy cauliflowers and outsize cabbages – the perfect size for lahanodolmathes (stuffed cabbage leaves) – are arranged on the stalls, together with spinach, which is cooked with rice and dill, or combined with squid to make an unusual but very tasty dish.

The only spots of bright colour on the market stalls come from scarlet bunches of beetroot. The flavour of these vegetables can be a bit bland but, when roasted and served with a robust garlic sauce, skorthalia, they taste superb. Mussels, too, are a good buy in the winter. Cheap, yet full of flavour, they are transformed into exotic pilaffs.

Sundays find the kitchens filled with the aromas of delicious meat dishes. Stifatho, a slow-simmered stew with glazed pickling-size onions, which can be made with beef, rabbit or octopus, is a real favourite, as is pork cooked with chickpeas and orange, a dish that originated on the islands of the Aegean.

More time spent indoors means more time to devote to the kitchen, so this is the season when women willingly prepare laborious dishes like lahanodolmathes for the family to enjoy in the evening. Preparing, filling and layering the cigar-shaped parcels is a lengthy business, but word can always be sent to a friend or neighbour, who, in return for a kafethaki – a Greek coffee – and a lively chat, will happily spend the morning rolling cabbage leaves. When the dolmathes are safely bubbling on the stove, there is the pleasure of reading the coffee cups: coffee grounds in the shape of a boat means a journey, while dots suggest money.

**Winter ingredients** are in the comfort zone – pulses and warm spices for soups and casseroles designed to keep the cold at bay, plus tasty seafood for those occasions when you feel you deserve a special treat.

## Lentils

Native to the Mediterranean, lentils come in various sizes and colours. The ones most often used in Greece are grey-green. Large and small types are available, the smaller, rounder variety having the better flavour. Lentils cook quickly, have a nutty flavour and do not need to be soaked before being cooked. They are used to make a wonderful soup, which is often served on Friday, which is a fast day. They also make the traditional meal on Good Friday when they are simply boiled and served only with vinegar.

## Chickpeas

Like lentils, chickpeas come from the Mediterranean region and have been an important food for centuries. In ancient Greece they were served both as a savoury staple and as a dessert, when they were roasted. Their nutty, almost earthy flavour makes for wonderful casseroles, particularly when they are combined with pork or lamb. They have an affinity for lemon, and a little lemon juice added to chickpea soup will really lift the flavour. Chickpeas are also used to make spicy rissoles.

It is essential to soak chickpeas overnight before cooking them and then they need to be boiled for several hours, unless a pressure cooker is used, in which case they take only 20–25 minutes.

**Top left**
Most pulses need to be soaked overnight in cold water.

**Left**
Chickpeas have a nutty, slightly earthy flavour that goes well with lemon. They make wonderful casseroles and soups, and combined with spices and herbs can be made into rissoles.

**Opposite**
Clockwise from top left: favourite winter foods include red mullet baked with orange, almonds, cabbage leaves stuffed with flavourful rice mixtures, citrus fruits and baby onions – an essential ingredient in the delicious rich meaty stew, stifatho.

## Beans

There are numerous varieties of dried beans, the most popular in Greece being the slim, elongated cannellini bean. Unlike the broad bean, which is indigenous to the country, the cannellini bean comes from Argentina. Greeks have embraced it with enthusiasm, however, and it is the basis of fasolatha, the most Greek

of Greek dishes, a hearty soup that has nourished generations of Greeks through good times and bad. Cannellini beans are also combined with lamb or pork in slow-simmered stews. Also highly favoured are the huge, fleshy fasolia gigantes. These beans are cultivated in northern Greece, the best coming from Kastoria. When dried, they are used in soups, as purées, in casseroles and with meat and salads. Aside from their value in providing protein during the winter months, they are staple foods during periods of fasting, particularly Lent. Dried beans must be soaked overnight, then drained, rinsed and drained again before being used. It is essential to boil kidney beans hard for at least 10 minutes before simmering them, to eliminate toxins, and it is good practice to get into the habit of doing this with any type of dried bean.

The secret of the wonderful flavour of dried beans cooked Greek-style is generous amounts of the finest Greek olive oil, which really seems to bring out their taste.

## Squid and cuttlefish

These are very popular in Greece, especially during the winter months, when they are often fried to accompany frugal Greek dishes such as cannellini bean soup or wilted spinach with rice and dill. In addition, they are made into dishes in their own right, often with rice, spinach or potatoes.

If you buy squid or cuttlefish from the fishmonger, he or she will probably prepare it for you, given sufficient notice. However, there may be occasions when you need to prepare it yourself.

**Top left**
Big creamy gigantes beans, from Kastoria in northern Greece, are a staple food throughout the winter months.

**Far left**
Squid is extremely popular in Greece, quickly fried and eaten hot to accompany more frugal dishes like bean soups.

**Left**
Allspice, though not native to Greece, has become a favourite of Greek cooks, and is essential for marinades.

## Preparing squid and cuttlefish

- Wash the squid or cuttlefish carefully. If there is any ink on the body, rinse it off so that you can see what you are doing.
- Holding the body firmly, pull away the head and tentacles. If the ink sac is still intact, remove it. Either keep it for cooking or discard it.
- Pull out all the innards, including the long transparent stick or "pen".
- Peel off and discard the thin purple skin on the body, but keep the two small fins on the sides.
- Slice the head across just under the eyes, severing the tentacles. Discard the rest of the head. Squeeze the tentacles at the head end to push out the round beak in the centre. Throw this away.
- Rinse the pouch and the tentacles very thoroughly. Drain well.

- If the squid or cuttlefish is to be stuffed, leave the pouch whole. Alternatively, slice it into rings. The tentacles are often left whole for frying, but they can be chopped into short lengths if preferred.

**Above right**
Kefalotyri cheese, a hard Greek cheese that is made from either cow's or sheep's milk, has a wonderfully sharp flavour – athough its principal characteristic is its saltiness.

## Kefalotyri cheese

The main characteristic of kefalotyri, a hard cheese made from cow's or sheep's milk is its saltiness. It is traditionally the cheese that is grated over dishes such as yiouvetsi (baked lamb with pasta) and, because it does not become runny when cooked, may be fried to make tasty mezethes to serve with drinks.

## Graviera cheese

The best graviera is Cretan. It is made from sheep's milk and, when properly aged, is superb. Naxos graviera is milder, while dodoni, made from cow's milk, is quite sweet. Metsovo has an intriguing flavour and lathotiry mytilinis, aged in olive oil, has an attractive piquant taste.

## Allspice

This spice comes not from the Mediterranean, but from the West Indies. It is a favourite of the Greek islands, probably a remnant of their Venetian occupiers. Allspice berries can be used ground or – as is usually the case in Greece – whole. The flavour and aroma are like a combination of cloves, cinnamon, cardamom and nutmeg – hence the name.

2 medium slices of bread, crusts removed
500g/1¼lb minced (ground) lamb or beef
1 onion, grated
5ml/1 tsp each dried thyme and oregano
45ml/3 tbsp chopped fresh flat
    leaf parsley, plus extra to garnish
1 egg, lightly beaten
salt and ground black pepper
lemon wedges, to serve (optional)

**For frying**
25g/1oz/¼ cup plain (all-purpose) flour
30–45ml/2–3 tbsp vegetable oil

**Serves 4**

# fried meatballs
keftethes

No Greek celebration or party is complete
without keftethes. They are always a must on
the meze table, as they are so appetizing.
Alternatively, they make a luxurious addition
to a frugal meal, such as one of the hot
winter soups.

**1** Soak the slices of bread in a bowl of water for
about 10 minutes, then drain. With your hands,
squeeze the bread dry before placing it in a
large bowl.

**2** Add the meat, onion, dried herbs, parsley,
egg, salt and pepper to the bread. Mix together,
preferably using your hands, until well blended.

**3** Shape the meat mixture into walnut-size balls
and roll the balls in the flour to lightly coat them,
shaking off any excess.

**4** Heat the oil in a large frying pan. When it is
hot, add the meatballs and fry, turning them
frequently, until they are cooked through and
look crisp and brown all over. Lift out and drain
on a double sheet of kitchen paper, to get rid of
the excess oil. Sprinkle with chopped parsley
and serve with lemon wedges, if you like.

30ml/2 tbsp olive oil, for frying
8 slices Greek Kefalotyri or Greek Cypriot
    Haloumi cheese, each about
    1cm/½in thick
ground black pepper
lemon wedges, to serve

**For the salad**
15ml/1 tbsp red wine vinegar
60ml/4 tbsp extra virgin olive oil
a large handful of rocket (arugula) leaves

**Serves 4**

# fried cheese with rocket salad
saganaki

At metropolitan parties you may well be offered this as finger food, but there is also a more robust version, as served in tavernas or private homes. A small, blackened, cast-iron frying pan will be brought to the table, with the slices of cheese still sizzling in it. The traditional cheese is the Greek kefalotyri, which is rich and quite salty, so you need only allow a couple of slices per person.

**1** Start by making the salad. Whisk the vinegar and extra virgin olive oil in a bowl and dress the rocket leaves. Spread them out on a platter.

**2** Heat the olive oil for frying in a large griddle pan or non-stick frying pan and lay the slices of cheese, side by side, on the base. Do not allow the slices to touch as they might stick together. Let them sizzle for a couple of minutes, turning each one over using tongs or a metal spatula as it starts to get crisp at the sides.

**3** Sprinkle the cheese slices with pepper. As soon as the bases turn golden, remove them from the pan and arrange them on the dressed rocket. Serve immediately, with the lemon wedges to squeeze over the top.

675g/1½lb medium or small
  beetroot (beets)
75–90ml/5–6 tbsp extra virgin olive oil
salt

**For the garlic sauce**
4 medium slices of bread, crusts removed,
  soaked in water for 10 minutes
2–3 garlic cloves, chopped
15ml/1 tbsp white wine vinegar
60ml/4 tbsp extra virgin olive oil

**Serves 4**

# roasted beetroot with garlic sauce
## pantzaria me skorthalia

In Greece, beetroot is a favourite winter vegetable, either served solo as a salad or with a layer of the flavourful garlic sauce, known as skorthalia, on top. It is the combination of the concentrated sweetness of the beetroot with the sharpness of the sauce that I find irresistible. Skorthalia has been enjoyed by the Greeks for a long time. Today, it is served with fried fish or with vegetables such as beetroot or courgettes (zucchini). Although in Greece the beetroot would be boiled, I roast them for a more concentrated sweetness.

1 Preheat the oven to 180°C/350°F/Gas 4. Rinse the beetroot under running water to remove any grit, but be careful not to pierce the skin or the colour will run.

2 Line a roasting pan with a large sheet of foil and place the beetroot on top. Drizzle a little of the olive oil over them, sprinkle lightly with salt and fold over both edges of the foil to enclose the beetroot completely. Bake for about 1½ hours until perfectly soft.

3 While the beetroot are cooking, make the garlic sauce. Squeeze most of the water out of the bread, but leave it quite moist. Place it in a blender or food processor. Add the garlic and vinegar, with salt to taste, and blend until smooth.

4 While the blender or processor is running, drizzle in the olive oil through the lid or feeder tube. The sauce should be runny. Spoon it into a bowl and set it aside.

5 Remove the beetroot from the foil package. When they are cool enough to handle, peel them. Slice them in thin round slices and arrange on a flat platter. Drizzle the remaining oil all over. Either spread a thin layer of garlic sauce on top, or hand it around separately. Serve with fresh bread, if you like.

150ml/¼ pint/⅔ cup extra virgin olive oil,
  plus extra for serving
1 large onion, chopped
350g/12oz/1¾ cups dried chickpeas,
  soaked in cold water overnight
15ml/1 tbsp plain (all-purpose) flour
juice of 1 lemon, or more if needed
45ml/3 tbsp chopped fresh flat
  leaf parsley
salt and ground black pepper

**Serves 4**

# chickpea soup
revithia soupa

**This popular Greek winter staple remains one of my favourite soups. I enjoy it at any season, even in the hot summer months on the island of Alonnisos. Compared to other soups based on pulses, which are often very hearty, this has a unique lightness in terms of both flavour and texture. With fresh bread and feta cheese, it makes a delicious, healthy meal.**

**1** Heat the olive oil in a heavy pan, add the onion and sauté until it starts to colour. Meanwhile, drain the chickpeas, rinse them under cold water and drain them again. Shake the colander or sieve to dry the chickpeas as much as possible, then add them to the pan. Turn them with a spatula for a few minutes to coat them well in the oil, then pour in enough hot water to cover them by about 4cm/1½in.

**2** Bring to the boil. Skim off any white froth that rises to the surface, using a slotted spoon. Lower the heat, add some pepper, cover and cook for 1–1¼ hours or until the chickpeas are soft.

**3** Put the flour in a cup and stir in the lemon juice with a fork. When the chickpeas are perfectly soft, add this mixture to them. Mix well, then add salt and pepper to taste. Cover the pan and cook gently for 5–10 minutes more, stirring occasionally.

**4** To thicken the soup slightly, take out about two cupfuls of the chickpeas and put them in a food processor. Process briefly so that the chickpeas are broken up, but remain slightly rough. Stir into the soup in the pan and mix well. Add the parsley, then taste the soup. If it seems a little bland, add more lemon juice. Serve in heated bowls and offer extra olive oil at the table, for drizzling on top of the soup.

275g/10oz/1½ cups dried cannellini
  beans, soaked overnight in cold water
1 large onion, thinly sliced
1 celery stick, sliced
2–3 carrots, sliced in discs
400g/14oz can tomatoes
15ml/1 tbsp tomato purée (paste)
150ml/¼ pint/⅔ cup extra virgin olive oil
5ml/1 tsp dried oregano
30ml/2 tbsp finely chopped fresh flat
  leaf parsley
salt and ground black pepper

**Serves 4**

# cannellini bean soup
## fasolia soupa

If there were one dish with which the whole Greek nation would identify, it would be this one. From the largest cities to the smallest villages it remains the favourite. It is always served with bread and olives, and perhaps raw onion quarters (or raw garlic for those with robust palates). Pickled or salted fish are also traditional accompaniments. For a more substantial meal you could serve this soup with fried squid or keftethes.

**1** Drain the beans, rinse them under cold water and drain them again. Tip them into a large pan, pour in enough water to cover and bring to the boil. Cook for about 3 minutes, then drain.

**2** Return the beans to the pan, pour in fresh water to cover them by about 3cm/1¼in, then add the onion, celery, carrots and tomatoes, and stir in the tomato purée, olive oil and oregano. Season with a little pepper, but don't add salt at this stage, as it would toughen the skins of the beans.

**3** Bring to the boil, lower the heat and cook for about 1 hour, until the beans are just tender. Season with salt, stir in the parsley and serve.

200g/7oz/1¼ cups mixed beans
  and lentils
25g/1oz/2 tbsp whole wheat grains
150ml/¼ pint/⅔ cup extra virgin olive oil
1 large onion, finely chopped
2 garlic cloves, crushed
5–6 fresh sage leaves, chopped
juice of 1 lemon
3 spring onions (scallions), thinly sliced
60–75ml/4–5 tbsp chopped fresh dill
salt and ground black pepper

**Serves 4**

# braised beans and lentils
cretan pallikaria

I was served this dish once at a lovely dinner in Crete. It's wonderfully easy to make, but it is vital that you start soaking the pulses and wheat the day before you want to serve the dish. Offer some tasty olive oil at the table, so guests can drizzle a little oil over their food.

**1** Put the pulses and wheat in a large bowl and cover with cold water. Leave to soak overnight.

**2** Next day, drain the pulse mixture, rinse it under cold water and drain again. Put the mixture in a large pan. Cover with plenty of cold water and cook for about 1½ hours, by which time all the ingredients will be quite soft. Strain, reserving 475ml/16fl oz/2 cups of the cooking liquid. Return the bean mixture to the clean pan.

**3** Heat the oil in a frying pan and fry the onion until light golden. Add the garlic and sage. As soon as the garlic becomes aromatic, add the mixture to the beans. Stir in the reserved liquid, add plenty of seasoning and simmer for about 15 minutes, or until the pulses are piping hot. Stir in the lemon juice, then spoon into serving bowls, top with a sprinkling of spring onions and dill and serve.

675g/1½lb fresh spinach, trimmed of any
    hard stalks
105ml/7 tbsp extra virgin olive oil
1 large onion, chopped
juice of ½ lemon
150ml/¼ pint/⅔ cup water
115g/4oz/generous ½ cup long grain rice
45ml/3 tbsp chopped fresh dill, plus extra
    sprigs to garnish
salt and ground black pepper

**Serves 4 as a main course**
**6 as a first course**

# wilted spinach with rice and dill
spanakorizo

**Spinach and rice makes a very successful combination. This is a delicious, yet frugal dish that can be made in very little time. In Greece it is particularly popular during periods of fasting, when meat is avoided for religious reasons. Serve it as a main course with some fried fish or chickpea rissoles.**

**1** Thoroughly wash the spinach in several changes of cold water until clean, then drain it in a colander. Shake off the excess water and shred the spinach coarsely.

**2** Heat the olive oil in a large pan and sauté the onion until translucent. Add the spinach and stir for a few minutes to coat it with the oil.

**3** As soon as the spinach looks wilted, add the lemon juice and the measured water and bring to the boil. Add the rice and half of the dill, then cover and cook gently for about 10 minutes or until the rice is cooked to your taste. If it looks too dry, add a little hot water.

**4** Spoon into a serving dish and sprinkle the little sprigs of dill over the top. Serve hot or at room temperature.

75–90ml/5–6 tbsp extra virgin olive oil
1 medium cauliflower, divided into
    large florets
2 eggs
juice of 1 lemon
5ml/1 tsp cornflour (cornstarch), mixed to
    a cream with a little cold water
30ml/2 tbsp chopped fresh flat
    leaf parsley
salt

**Serves 4 as a main course
6 as a first course**

# cauliflower with egg and lemon
kounoupithi avgolemono

Cauliflower has a bit of a bad image but, if
you treat it well, it can be quite rewarding. In
Greece it is very popular and is used in a
number of different ways. Here it is teamed
with a lemon sauce. Try serving it with
something rich and appetizing, such as
keftethes (fried meatballs).

**1** Heat the olive oil in a large heavy pan, add
the cauliflower florets and sauté over a medium
heat until they start to brown.

**2** Pour in enough hot water to almost cover the
cauliflower, add salt to taste, then cover the pan
and cook for 7–8 minutes until the florets are just
soft. Remove the pan from the heat and leave to
stand, covered, while you make the sauce.

**3** Beat the eggs in a bowl, add the lemon juice
and cornflour and beat until well mixed. While
beating, add a few tablespoons of the hot liquid
from the cauliflower. Pour the egg mixture slowly
over the cauliflower, then stir gently. Place the
pan over a very gentle heat for 2 minutes to
thicken the sauce. Spoon into a warmed serving
bowl, sprinkle the chopped parsley over the top
and serve.

1 white cabbage
12 black olives

**For the vinaigrette**
75–90ml/5–6 tbsp extra virgin olive oil
30ml/2 tbsp lemon juice
1 garlic clove, crushed
30ml/2 tbsp finely chopped fresh flat
   leaf parsley
salt

**Serves 4**

# cabbage salad with lemon vinaigrette and black olives
lahano salata

In winter, lahano salata frequently appears on the Greek table. It is made with compact creamy-coloured "white" cabbage. In more northern climates, this type of tight-headed cabbage tends to be a little woody, but in Greece, it always produces a rather sweet tasting, unusual salad, which has a crisp and refreshing texture.

**1** Cut the cabbage in quarters, discard the outer leaves and trim off any thick, hard stems as well as the hard base.

**2** Lay each quarter in turn on its side and cut long, very thin slices until you reach the central core, which should be discarded. The key to a perfect cabbage salad is to shred the cabbage as finely as possible. Place the shredded cabbage in a bowl and stir in the black olives.

**3** Make the vinaigrette by whisking the olive oil, lemon juice, garlic, parsley and salt together in a bowl until well blended. Pour the dressing over the salad, and toss the cabbage and olives until everything is evenly coated.

275g/10oz/1½ cups black-eyed
  beans (peas)
5 spring onions (scallions), sliced
a large handful of rocket (arugula) leaves,
  chopped if large
45–60ml/3–4 tbsp chopped fresh dill
150ml/¼ pint/⅔ cup extra virgin olive oil
juice of 1 lemon, or more
10–12 black olives
salt and ground black pepper
small cos (romaine) lettuce leaves, to
  serve (optional)

**Serves 4**

# warm black-eyed bean salad with rocket

mavromatika fasolia salata

**This is an easy dish as black-eyed beans do not need to be soaked overnight. By adding spring onions and loads of aromatic dill, it is transformed to a refreshing and healthy dish. It can be served hot or at room temperature.**

**1** Rinse and drain the beans, tip them into a pan and pour in cold water to cover. Bring to the boil and immediately strain. Put them back in the pan with fresh cold water to cover and add a pinch of salt – this will make their skins harder and stop them from disintegrating when they are cooked.

**2** Bring the beans to the boil, then lower the heat slightly and cook them until they are soft but not mushy. They will take 20–30 minutes, so keep an eye on them.

**3** Drain the beans, reserving 75–90ml/5–6 tbsp of the cooking liquid. Tip the beans into a large salad bowl. Immediately add the remaining ingredients, including the reserved liquid, and mix well. Serve straightaway, or leave to cool slightly and serve with lettuce, if you like.·

1kg/2¼lb fresh squid
120ml/4fl oz/½ cup extra virgin olive oil
1 large onion, sliced
3 spring onions (scallions), chopped
1 glass white wine, about 175ml/6fl oz/
  ¾ cup
150ml/¼ pint/⅔ cup hot water
500g/1¼lb fresh spinach
juice of ½ lemon
45ml/3 tbsp chopped fresh dill
salt and ground black pepper
chunks of fresh bread, to serve

**Serves 4**

# squid with spinach
kalamarakia me horta

**This is an unusual dish, which is occasionally made on the island of Crete. It is absolutely delicious and should be made more often.**

**1** Prepare the squid, following the instructions in the introduction to this chapter. Slice the body into half vertically, then slice into 1cm/½in strips. Cut each tentacle into smaller pieces.

**2** Heat the oil in a wide, heavy pan and sauté the onion slices and spring onions until the onion slices are translucent. Increase the heat and add the squid. It will produce some moisture, but keep stirring and the moisture will evaporate. Continue to stir for 10 minutes more, or until the squid starts to turn golden.

**3** Pour in the wine, let it evaporate, then add the hot water, with salt and pepper to taste. Cover the pan and cook for about 30 minutes, stirring occasionally.

**4** Rinse and drain the spinach, chop it coarsely and stir it into the pan. When it starts to wilt, cover and cook for about 10 minutes. Just before serving, add the lemon juice and dill and mix well. Serve with fresh bread.

a few sprigs of fresh dill
4 large red mullet, total weight
    1–1.2kg/2¼–2½lb, cleaned
2 large oranges, halved
½ lemon
60ml/4 tbsp extra virgin olive oil
30ml/2 tbsp pine nuts
salt

**Serves 4**

# baked red mullet with oranges
barbounia sto fourno me portokali

Oranges are so plentiful in Greece that they can be picked from trees in the streets. The aroma of orange zest pervades many of the Greek's classic dishes, and the juice adds flavour to wonderful recipes like this one.

**1** Place some fresh dill in the cavity of each fish and lay them in a baking dish, preferably one that can be taken straight to the table.

**2** Set half an orange aside and squeeze the rest, along with the lemon. Mix the juice with the olive oil, then pour the mixture over the fish. Turn the fish so that they are evenly coated in the marinade, then cover and leave in a cool place to marinate for 1–2 hours, spooning the marinade over the fish occasionally.

**3** Preheat the oven to 180°C/350°F/Gas 4. Sprinkle a little salt over each fish. Slice the reserved half orange into thin rounds, then cut each round into quarters. Place two or three of these orange wedges over each fish. Bake for 20 minutes, then remove the dish from the oven, baste the fish with the juices and sprinkle the pine nuts over. Return the dish to the oven and bake for 10–15 minutes more.

2 octopuses, total weight about
  675–800g/1½–1¾lb, cleaned
150ml/¼ pint/⅔ cup extra virgin olive oil
2 large onions, sliced
3 garlic cloves, chopped
1 fresh red or green chilli, seeded
  and thinly sliced
1–2 bay leaves
5ml/1 tsp dried oregano
1 piece of cinnamon stick
2–3 grains allspice (optional)
1 glass red wine, 175ml/6fl oz/¾ cup
30ml/2 tbsp tomato purée (paste) diluted
  in 300ml/½ pint/1¼ cups warm water
300ml/½ pint/1¼ cups boiling water
225g/8oz/2 cups penne or small dried
  macaroni-type pasta
ground black pepper
45ml/3 tbsp finely chopped fresh flat
  leaf parsley, to garnish (optional)

**Serves 4**

# octopus and pasta bake
htapothi me makaronaki

**A mouthwatering and very unusual dish, this slow-cooked combination of octopus and pasta in a spicy tomato sauce is quite an everyday affair in Greece, but when we make it for our English friends it always creates a sensation. We like to serve it at winter dinner parties, when it reminds us of the particularly delicious version we often enjoy on our summer visits to the Olive Grove Restaurant at the dazzling beach of Lefto Yialo, where occasionally they make it with cuttlefish instead.**

**1** Rinse the octopuses well, making sure that there is no sand left in the suckers. Cut the octopuses into large cubes using a sharp knife and place the pieces in a heavy pan over a low heat. Cook gently; they will produce some liquid, the colour of the flesh will change and they will eventually become bright scarlet. Keep turning the pieces of octopus with a wooden spatula until all the liquid has evaporated.

**2** Add the olive oil to the pan and sauté the octopus pieces for 4–5 minutes. Add the onions to the pan and cook for a further 4–5 minutes, stirring them constantly until they start to turn golden.

**3** Stir in the garlic, chilli, bay leaf, oregano, cinnamon stick and allspice, if using. As soon as the garlic becomes aromatic, pour in the wine and let it bubble and evaporate for a couple of minutes.

**4** Pour in the diluted tomato purée, add some black pepper, cover and cook gently for 1½ hours or until the octopus is perfectly soft. Stir occasionally and add a little hot water if needed. The dish can be prepared up to this stage well in advance of serving.

**5** Preheat the oven to 160°C/325°F/Gas 3. Bring the octopus mixture to the boil, add the boiling water and stir in the dried pasta. Tip the mixture into a large roasting dish and level the surface. Transfer to the oven and bake for 30–35 minutes, stirring occasionally and adding a little hot water if the mixture starts to look dry. Sprinkle the parsley on top, if using, and serve.

### Cooking octopus
Do not add salt to octopus as it makes it tough and indigestible. The octopus mixture can be cooked in a pressure cooker, if you prefer. It will take 20 minutes under full pressure.

1.6kg/3½lb mussels, scrubbed and bearded
2 onions, thinly sliced
2 glasses white wine, about 350ml/
    12fl oz/1½ cups
450ml/¾ pint/scant 2 cups hot water
150ml/¼ pint/⅔ cup extra virgin olive oil
5–6 spring onions (scallions), chopped
2 garlic cloves, chopped
large pinch of dried oregano
200g/7oz/1 cup long grain rice
45ml/3 tbsp finely chopped fresh flat
    leaf parsley
45–60ml/3–4 tbsp chopped fresh dill
salt and ground black pepper

**Serves 4 as a main course
6 as a first course**

# mussel and rice pilaff
mithia pilafi

**This is a classic dish and a favourite one in Greece. It has layers of tastes and the herbs add enticing aromas. Although it is made with frugal ingredients (in Greece, mussels are cheap compared to fish) it always produces spectacular results and is well worth the time it takes to prepare the seafood.**

**1** Having prepared the mussels, discard any that are not tightly shut, or which fail to snap shut when tapped. Place the remainder in a large heavy pan. Add about one-third of the onion slices, then pour in half the wine and 150ml/¼ pint/⅔ cup of the hot water. Cover and cook over a high heat for about 5 minutes, shaking the pan occasionally, until the mussels start to open.

**2** Place a colander on top of a large bowl and, using a slotted spoon, transfer the open mussels to the colander so all their liquid collects in the bowl. Discard any mussels that remain closed. Shell most of the mussels, discarding their shells, but keep a dozen or so large ones in their shells for decorative purposes.

**3** Line a sieve with fine muslin or kitchen paper and place it over a large bowl. Let the liquid remaining in the pan settle, then strain it carefully through the lined sieve. Do the same with the liquid from the bowl, which drained from the cooked mussels.

**4** Heat the olive oil in a heavy deep pan or sauté pan, add the remaining onion slices and the spring onions and sauté over a medium heat until both start to turn golden. Add the garlic and the oregano.

**5** As soon as the garlic becomes aromatic, add the rice and stir briefly to coat the grains in the oil. Add the remaining wine, stirring until it has been absorbed, then stir in the remaining 300ml/½ pint/1¼ cups water, the reserved mussel liquid and the chopped parsley. Season with salt and pepper, then cover and cook gently for about 5 minutes, stirring occasionally.

**6** Add the mussels, including the ones in their shells. Sprinkle in half the dill and mix well. If necessary, add a little more hot water. Cover and cook gently for 5–6 minutes more, until the rice is cooked but still has a bit of bite at the centre of the grain.

**7** Sprinkle the remaining dill on top and serve with a green salad or cabbage salad with black olives.

1 organic or free-range chicken, about
  1.6kg/3½lb
2 garlic cloves, peeled, but left whole
15ml/1 tbsp chopped fresh thyme or
  oregano, or 5ml/1 tsp dried, plus
  2–3 fresh sprigs of thyme or oregano
800g/1¾lb potatoes
juice of 1 lemon
60ml/4 tbsp extra virgin olive oil
300ml/½ pint/1¼ cups hot water
salt and ground black pepper

**Serves 4**

# roast chicken with potatoes and lemon

kotopoulo fournou me patates

**This is a lovely, easy dish for a family meal. As with other Greek roasts, everything is baked together so that the potatoes absorb all the different flavours, especially that of the lemon.**

**1** Preheat the oven to 200°C/400°F/Gas 6. Place the chicken, breast side down, in a large roasting pan, then tuck the garlic cloves and the thyme or oregano sprigs inside the bird.

**2** Peel the potatoes and quarter them lengthways. If they are very large, slice them lengthways into thinner pieces. Arrange the potatoes around the chicken, then pour the lemon juice over the chicken and potatoes. Season with salt and pepper, drizzle the olive oil over the top and add about three-quarters of the chopped fresh or dried thyme or oregano. Pour the hot water into the roasting pan.

**3** Roast the chicken and potatoes for 30 minutes, then remove the roasting pan from the oven and carefully turn the chicken over. Season the bird with a little more salt and pepper, sprinkle over the remaining fresh or dried herbs, and add more hot water, if needed. Reduce the oven temperature to 190°C/375°F/Gas 5.

**4** Return the chicken and potatoes to the oven and roast them for another hour, or slightly longer, by which time both the chicken and the potatoes will be a golden colour. Serve with a crisp leafy salad.

75ml/5 tbsp olive oil
1kg/2¼lb good stewing or braising
   steak, cut in large cubes
3 garlic cloves, chopped
5ml/1 tsp ground cumin
5cm/2in piece of cinnamon stick
1 glass red wine, 175ml/6fl oz/¾ cup
30ml/2 tbsp red wine vinegar
small fresh rosemary sprig
2 bay leaves, crumbled
30ml/2 tbsp tomato purée (paste) diluted
   in 1 litre/1¾ pints/4 cups hot water
675g/1½lb small pickling-size onions,
   peeled and left whole
15ml/1 tbsp demerara (raw) sugar
salt and ground black pepper

**Serves 4**

# beef casserole with baby onions and red wine
moshari stifatho

This is the perfect Sunday lunch for a family, but is also an excellent choice for a dinner party. Moshari stifatho is an unusual but mouthwatering dish, with the small pickling-size onions melting in the mouth with sweetness. In Greece a stifatho is occasionally also made with rabbit or octopus. This is the kind of easy dish that can be left simmering slowly in the oven for hours without coming to any harm. Serve it with boiled rice, pasta, creamy mashed potatoes or fried potatoes.

**1** Heat the olive oil in a large heavy pan and brown the meat cubes, in batches if necessary, until pale golden brown all over.

**2** Stir in the garlic and cumin. Add the cinnamon stick and cook for a few seconds, then pour the wine and vinegar slowly over the mixture. Let the liquid bubble and evaporate for 3–4 minutes.

**3** Add the rosemary and bay leaves, with the diluted tomato purée. Stir well, season with salt and pepper, then cover and simmer gently for about 1½ hours or until the meat is tender.

**4** Dot the onions over the meat mixture and shake the pan to distribute them evenly. Sprinkle the demerara sugar over the onions, cover the pan and cook very gently for 30 minutes, until the onions are soft but have not begun to disintegrate. If necessary, add a little hot water at this stage. Do not stir once the onions have been added but gently shake the pan instead to coat them in the sauce. Remove the cinnamon stick and sprig of rosemary and serve.

### Using the oven instead

Stifatho can be cooked in the oven, if you prefer. Use a flameproof casserole. Having browned the meat and added the remaining ingredients, with the exception of the onions and sugar, transfer the covered casserole to an oven preheated to 160°C/325°F/Gas 3 and bake for about 2 hours, or until the meat is tender. Add the onions and sugar as above and return the casserole to the oven for 1 hour more.

350g/12oz/1¾ cups dried chickpeas,
   soaked overnight in water to cover
75–90ml/5–6 tbsp extra virgin olive oil
675g/1½lb boneless leg of pork, cut
   into large cubes
1 large onion, sliced
2 garlic cloves, chopped
400g/14oz can chopped tomatoes
grated rind of 1 orange
1 small dried red chilli
salt and ground black pepper

**Serves 4**

# pork with chickpeas and orange
revithia me hirino ke portokali

This winter speciality is a familiar dish in the Aegean islands, particularly in Crete. In the villages of Mesara it is traditionally offered to family and close friends on the night before a wedding. This version comes from the island of Chios. All you need to serve with this lovely dish is fresh bread and a bowl of black olives.

**1** Drain the chickpeas, rinse them under cold water and drain them again. Place them in a large, heavy pan. Pour in enough cold water to cover generously, put a lid on the pan and bring to the boil.

**2** Skim the surface, replace the lid and cook gently for 1–1½ hours, depending on the age and pedigree of the chickpeas. Alternatively, cook them in a pressure cooker for 20 minutes under full pressure. When the chickpeas are soft, drain them, reserving the cooking liquid, and set them aside.

**3** Heat the olive oil in the clean pan and brown the meat cubes in batches. As each cube browns, lift it out with a slotted spoon and put it on a plate. When all the meat cubes have been browned, add the onion to the oil remaining in the pan and sauté the slices until light golden. Stir in the garlic, then as soon as it becomes aromatic, add the tomatoes and orange rind.

**4** Crumble in the chilli. Return the chickpeas and meat to the pan, and pour in enough of the reserved cooking liquid to cover. Add the black pepper, but not salt at this stage.

**5** Mix well, cover the pan and simmer for about 1 hour, until the meat is tender. Stir occasionally and add more of the reserved liquid if needed. The result should be a moist casserole; not soupy, but not dry either. Season with salt before serving.

115g/4oz/generous ½ cup long grain rice
1–2 large green cabbages, total weight
    about 1.6–2kg/3½–4½lb
500g/1¼lb minced (ground) pork, or a
    mixture of pork and beef
1 large onion, roughly grated
1 egg, lightly beaten
30ml/2 tbsp chopped fresh flat leaf parsley
45–60ml/3–4 tbsp chopped fresh dill
90ml/6 tbsp extra virgin olive oil
25g/1oz/2 tbsp butter
15ml/1 tbsp cornflour (cornstarch)
2 eggs
juice of 1½ lemons
salt and ground black pepper

**Serves 4**

# stuffed cabbage leaves
lahanodolmathes

**This is the most enticing of the winter meals, and a real favourite of mine. However it is time-consuming to make. If you can enlist some help, it will make the task less onerous.**

1 Soak the rice in cold water for 10 minutes, then drain, rinse it under cold water and drain again. Core the cabbages and strip off the outer leaves. Rinse these and set aside. Peel off the inner leaves, cutting off more of the core as you proceed. When you reach the hard heart, stop peeling. Set the cabbage hearts aside.

2 Rinse the leaves and cabbage hearts in cold water, then drain them. Bring a large saucepan of water to the boil and blanch the leaves in batches for 1–2 minutes, until they become just pliable. Remove with a draining spoon and place them in a colander. Put in the cabbage hearts and let them boil for slightly longer. Drain.

3 Prepare the stuffing by combining the minced meat, rice, onion, egg and fresh herbs in a bowl. Mix in half the olive oil and a generous amount of seasoning. Cut the larger leaves of the cabbage in half and trim any hard cores and veins. Place about 15ml/1 tbsp of the stuffing at one end of a leaf, fold the end of the leaf over so it looks like a short fat cigar, then fold in the sides and roll up fairly tightly to make a neat package.

4 Carefully strip as many leaves as possible from the blanched cabbage heart and stuff them individually. Leave the inner heart intact, but open the leaves on the top, and put some stuffing in it, too.

5 Line a large heavy pan with the uncooked outer leaves. Layer the dolmathes in the pan, packing them tightly together. Season each layer as you go, then drizzle the remaining olive oil over the top and scatter over small knobs of the butter.

6 Invert a small heatproof plate on top of the last layer of dolmathes. Pour in enough hot water to just cover the top layer. Cover and cook gently for about 50 minutes. As soon as the dolmathes are cooked, tilt the pan, holding the plate down firmly, and empty most of the liquid into a bowl. Let it cool slightly.

7 Mix the cornflour to a cream with a little water. Whisk the eggs in another bowl, then add the lemon juice and the cornflour mixture and whisk again. Continue to whisk, gradually adding tablespoons of the hot cooking liquid from the dolmathes. As soon as the liquid has all been added, pour the sauce over the dolmathes and shake the pan gently to distribute it evenly. Return the pan to a very gentle heat and cook for 3 minutes to thicken the sauce, rotating the pan occasionally.

2.5ml/½ tsp bicarbonate of soda
  (baking soda)
grated rind and juice of 1 large orange
150ml/¼ pint/⅔ cup extra virgin olive oil
75g/3oz/6 tbsp caster (superfine) sugar
60ml/4 tbsp brandy
7.5ml/1½ tsp ground cinnamon
400g/14oz/3½ cups self-raising (self-rising)
  flour sifted with a pinch of salt
115g/4oz/1 cup shelled walnuts, chopped

**For the syrup**
225g/8oz/1 cup clear honey
115g/4oz/½ cup caster (superfine) sugar

**Makes 20**

# christmas honey cookies
melomakarona

**Christmas would lose some of its lustre for me without honey-coated melomakarona.**

**1** Mix together the baking soda and orange juice. Beat the oil and sugar with an electric mixer until blended. Beat in the brandy and 2.5ml/½ tsp of the cinnamon, then the orange juice and soda. Using your hand, gradually work the flour and salt into the mixture. As soon as it becomes possible to do so, knead it. Add the orange rind and knead for 10 minutes or until the dough is soft and pliable.

**2** Preheat the oven to 180°C/350°F/Gas 4. Flour your hands and pinch off small pieces of the dough. Shape them into 6cm/2½in long ovals and place on ungreased baking sheets. Using a fork dipped in water, flatten each cookie a little. Bake for 25 minutes, until golden. Cool slightly, then transfer to a wire rack to harden.

**3** Meanwhile, make the syrup. Place the honey, sugar and 150ml/¼ pint/⅔ cup water in a small pan. Bring gently to the boil, skim, then lower the heat and simmer for 5 minutes. Immerse the cold melomakarona about six at a time into the hot syrup and leave them for 1–2 minutes.

**4** Lift them out with a slotted spoon and place on a platter in a single layer. Sprinkle with the walnuts and remaining cinnamon.

225g/8oz/1 cup unsalted butter
150g/5oz/⅔ cup caster (superfine) sugar
2 egg yolks
5ml/1 tsp vanilla essence (extract)
2.5ml/½ tsp bicarbonate of soda
   (baking soda)
45ml/3 tbsp brandy
500g/1¼lb/5 cups plain (all-purpose) flour
   sifted with a pinch of salt
150g/5oz/1¼ cups blanched almonds,
   toasted and coarsely chopped
350g/12oz/3 cups icing (confectioners')
   sugar

**Makes 20–22**

# butter and almond shortbreads
kourabiethes

**Dazzling white kourabiethes are traditionally made at Christmas and Easter, but are also an important feature of many other Greek celebrations. They are traditionally crescent-shaped, but I have cut them into stars.**

**1** Cream the butter, beat in the caster sugar gradually, until light and fluffy. Beat in the egg yolks one at a time, then the vanilla. Mix the soda with the brandy and stir into the mixture. Add the flour and salt and mix to a firm dough. Knead lightly, add the almonds and knead again.

**2** Preheat the oven to 180°C/350°F/Gas 4. Cover half the dough with clear film (plastic wrap) and set aside. Roll out the remaining dough until about 2.5cm/1in thick. Press out star or half-moon shapes, using pastry cutters. Repeat with the remaining dough. Place on the baking sheets and bake for 20–25 minutes, or until pale golden. Do not let them brown.

**3** Meanwhile, sift a quarter of the icing sugar on to a platter. As soon as the kourabiethes come out of the oven, dust them generously with icing sugar. Let them cool for a few minutes, then place them on the sugar-coated platter.

**4** Sift the remaining icing sugar over them. The aim is to give them a generous coating, so they are pure white.

## Author's acknowledgements

Writing a book, particularly a book about food in a certain country, is like a journey – never without companions. There are many people who have accompanied me on this particular journey and I am indebted to a number of them, but the cooks first. Vlassis of the eponymous restaurant in Athens who has been an inspiration to me, not only with his wonderful cooking, but also with his approach to food and the way he serves it in his restaurant. Magna Anagnostou of The Olive Grove restaurant in Alonnisos, who is one of the most enthusiastic cooks I know; Anna Anagnostou of The Meltemi restaurant and her mother Maria Karakatsani, who make the best imam bayildi; and my friend Magda Besini who cooks the most wonderful goat yiouvetsi and the best cheese pies.

I'd also like to thank my sisters, Maria Fokianidou and Sally Printziou, who live in Athens, for cooking and sharing lovely meals with me; and my friends Manuela Pandazithou-Selleli and Katy Spyraki, who are always ready to try everything; Maria Pandazithou in Crete for her hospitality; and Anna and Elia Psarrea in Volos for both their hospitality and their novel seafood dishes.

I am grateful, too, to my editor Linda Fraser for such a beautifully conceived book and for her sensitive approach to this project, Martin Brigdale for his stunning photographs, my agent Caroline Davidson for her hard work, and, of course, to my husband Graeme and my lovely daughters, Alexandra and Sophie, for being such enthusiastic eaters.

## Publisher's acknowledgements

And the journey did, of course, continue for a while after Rena's testing and writing were complete. We would like to thank the photographer, Martin Brigdale, and Helen Trent, the props stylist, for creating such fabulous recipe pictures, Lucy McKelvie and Linda Tubby for their brilliant food styling and, finally, Jenni Fleetwood for her excellent editing.

## Picture acknowledgements

All photographs are by Martin Brigdale; although the location pictures on page 8 (top right) and 9 were supplied by the Anthony Blake Photo Library.

First published by Aquamarine in 2001
© Anness Publishing Limited 2001

Aquamarine is an imprint of
Anness Publishing Limited
Hermes House, 88–89 Blackfriars Road
London SE1 8HA

All rights reserved. No part of this publication may be reproduced, stored in a retrieval system, or transmitted in any way or by any other means, electronic, mechanical, photocopying, recording or otherwise, without the prior written permission of the copyright holder.

A CIP catalogue record for this book is available from the British Library

Publisher: Joanna Lorenz
Managing Editor: Linda Fraser
Copy Editor: Jenni Fleetwood
Production Controller: Claire Rae
Editorial Reader: Joy Wotton
Photographer: Martin Brigdale
Designer: Anita Schnable
Stylist: Helen Trent
Home Economists: Lucy McKelvie and
    Linda Tubby
Indexer: Hilary Bird
Typesetter: Diane Pullen

## Notes

Bracketed terms are intended for American readers. For all recipes, quantities are given in both metric and imperial measures and, where appropriate, measures are also given in standard cups and spoons. Follow one set, but not a mixture, because they are not interchangeable. Standard spoon and cup measures are level. 1 tsp = 5ml, 1 tbsp = 15ml, 1 cup = 250ml/8fl oz. Australian standard tablespoons are 20ml. Australian readers should use 3 tsp in place of 1 tbsp for measuring small quantities of flour, salt, etc. Medium (US large) eggs are used unless otherwise stated.